Carolina Country

READER

James A. Chaney, Editor

Moore Publishing Company
Durham, North Carolina

Library of Congress Catalog Card No. 73-86780

ISBN 0-87716-045-7

*To Janie
and the memory of my
Mother and Father*

FOREWORD

"What lies beyond what we can see?"

Jim Chaney asks that question in the opening of *Carolina Country Reader*, and he then begins to tell us in some 250 delightful pages, in poignant pieces of nostalgia, perceptive insights into the human heart, and descriptions of the wonders that lie beyond the next hill or the next bend in the road.

Robert Frost talked about the two roads which diverged in a yellow wood and he was sorry that he could not travel both. Jim Chaney has traveled those roads, taking one and then doubling back to take the other, and he shares with us the wonders of the journey.

But beyond the physical places — and there are moving and beautiful descriptions of many Tar Heel scenes — Jim also knows the wisdom which lies in the statement by William Faulkner that the greatest story is in the human heart in conflict with itself. In this *Carolina Country Reader* there are many such stories — a child's hopes and dreams at Christmas time, a peace that comes with understanding between an old couple, and old neighbors.

Jim Chaney had established a solid reputation as one of North Carolina's best reporters long before he took over as editor of *Carolina Country* — and he writes with the reporter's trained eyes and ears, but he also writes with wonder. He writes as if seeing this place for the first time and the reader shares his wonder in what he sees.

He delves into history as well into the lives of people, and he sees physical places as not just a point on a map or a listing in a geography book but as a place where people live. The human touch is evident on every page.

Most of the pieces in this book are by Jim Chaney, but there are also contributions from such well known writers as Guy Owen; Lodwick Hartley, who tells about his experiences with wildlife in "The Animal Kingdom"; Lucy Daniels Inman, who has a wonderful recollection of Christmas with her grandparents; Bryan Haislip, who tells of the marvel of electricity coming to a North Carolina farm; J.C. Brown, Jr., telling the story of "The Five-String Banjo"; Ed Brown, Jr., and Richard Pence.

The result is a collection to delight any reader of any age at any place. The book directs its attention to North Carolina but its themes are universal. Dip into it on any page and there will be prose or poetry which will touch the memory or the heart. There will be laughter, too, for there is wit and humor running as a silver thread through this narrative portrait of a time and a place and a people.

Carolina Country Reader can be read at one sitting, but we recommend a slow savoring of its contents. There are places you will want to read aloud to someone close to you, and there are others you will want to peruse and ponder upon alone. It is a book which pays attention to the seasons — the human seasons as well as the turns of the calendar. Indeed it is a Book for All Seasons.

Sam Ragan

CONTENTS

Carolina Country

READER

WHAT LIES BEYOND WHAT WE CAN SEE?

Along the highway as US 1 runs north to Henderson, the woods stand back to give a pasture room, and there across a rounded hill a path meanders as if to show a straight line is not the natural course.

Where, if you could follow the path, would you find the end of it? A path which looks so much used surely would not stop just beyond the hilltop. But as you pass you see no trace of it on the shoulders of the hill beyond.

And what of the other mysteries beside the other roads you travel?

If you could stop and ask at the old houses that catch your eye, would you be invited in if you said your only reason was curiosity?

If you turned down the road marked Pocomoke, would you really come to such a place? Or is it, like Wake County's Hurricane, a place often mentioned but which you have never found?

If you paused where the pines stand tall and clean of underbrush along US 64 westward and beyond a bridge, would you find the cool tranquility to be only an illusion?

One day, sometime, you say. The next time I come this way.

Perhaps if we leave early enough so that we could stop for a few minutes. . . if we come this way again. . . Perhaps. . .

But of course you never do.

And the valleys keep their secrets and the side roads are never explored, and the old houses and the pine grove are like the path across the pasture.

1

Somewhere, perhaps beyond the rounded hill, it reaches a place, this path, where there is nothing more to lead to and where there is no coming back.

And perhaps as we hurry by, wondering but never stopping to see for sure, looking but going too swiftly to really absorb, we are following such a path.

Perhaps all our lives are merely meanderings through such a pasture, to a destination which none of us can really know until we have stopped long enough to consider where it is we really want to go and have climbed high enough to see beyond the hill.

FEBRUARY'S SECRET

Can you believe in February? Can
    you count
On a month that routs groundhogs
    out
To tell, as if groundhogs knew,
    how long
Winter has to stay? Or if there are
Signs of spring so early?
As if a shadow could cost six
    weeks more
Of burrowing through sleet and
    snow
Until bare branches sprout fresh
    buds
And jonquils peep above the
    ground to see
If the japonica is budding yet.
What does February know of
    spring?
And if it knew,
Would the jonquils tell?

IF THE WIFE IS WATCHING

You may have thought you had to have a garden to grow vegetables. If you still do, it's because you haven't been reading what the seed companies are saying.

The way they tell it, you can buy their seeds and grow vegetables in a flower box or in a can of dirt, or any place you can grow a flower.

Think of it a little, and all sorts of possibilities will come to mind for you, just as they have for the seed companies.

If you have a vine entwining a fence, you could have cucumbers there, growing with their fruit hanging handy to pick like grapes on an arbor. If you have a flower bed, you can grow lettuce around it as a border. And you can grow peppers as you might grow pansies, radishes by the back steps and tomatoes on a trellis like roses.

Come to think of it, you might give up flowers altogether and just grow vegetables for decoration as well as eating.

You might, but you probably won't. In the first place, who is going to be watching when you start clearing out the zinnias to put in cabbages, and pulling up the pansies to put in peppers, or rooting out the thrift to make way for lettuce? Nine times out of ten, it will be the wife. And with her watching, how many peppers do you think will replace pansies?

Dig up those zinnias, she'll say, and you'll be cooking your cabbages yourself.

Well, that's the way it is, and that's another battle lost. It's been that way, you can bet, ever since man and woman got the first seed from that first apple. And if the seed companies think they can change it, they don't know Eve.

WHAT DOCTORS DON'T KNOW
... NOR PARENTS EITHER

What you do when you have the measles is plug up your nose.

Maybe doctors don't know about that yet. A seven-year-old boy did, though.

Shortly after the rash appeared in a mass of red welts across his face, this young man plugged his nostrils with two wads of toilet paper. In spite of pleadings, warnings and reprimands, he continued to plug.

"It stops it from smelling bad," he insisted.

So maybe you didn't know the measles smell. Doctors don't say anything about the smell, not usually, in describing the symptoms to parents.

Children are the ones who know about such things.

"When I had my tonsils out," the little girl said, "I couldn't drink cocoa any more. I could before, but I can't any more."

"Eggs make me have chickenpox," the other little girl said. "I just had to stop eating them."

"Why is your arm in a cast, Billy?" the neighbor asked.

"The doctor had to put it there because I was swinging," Billy answered.

You fell? the neighbor asked.

"No," Billy answered. "Martha fell. I was swinging and Martha fell and the swing set turned over."

"We had the mumps at our house," the little girls reported proudly. "But my daddy can't have them. My mother said that's one thing she doesn't want daddy to share."

Medical science has accomplished wonders, but there are many things children know that still mystify the researchers, just as they do children's parents and children's doctors.

There was a child who insisted he had a bug in his ear. Wax, said his parents. Wax, said the doctor. But, of course, it was a bug.

"I'd never have believed it," the mother said when the doctor removed the bug.

"One of the things you learn practicing medicine," the doctor said, "is that nothing's unbelievable, especially not when a child's involved."

There was a cry from the bedroom in the hours between midnight and dawn.

"A spider's in my room," the child said.

"Of course not," his mother told him, "It's just a shadow. I don't see anything."

"But there is a spider," the child repeated.

And, of course, when mother turned on the lights, there it was: a harmless granddaddy longlegs, but a spider nevertheless.

"I'll never know how he saw it," she told her husband. "I couldn't see it until I turned on the lights."

"Take those wads out of your nose. They'll get stuck up there and we'll have to get a doctor to take them out," the boy's father demanded.

"If I do it will smell bad," the boy answered.

"Measles smell?" the father said. "How'd you get that notion?"

And when he pulled the child to him to pull out the nose stoppers, the father smelled this curious odor.

"He must need a bath," the father said.

"He's had a bath," said the mother.

Measles? Does it really smell like that?

"I know it must be hard treating children," the mother told the pediatrician. "Particularly infants. They can't tell

6

you what's wrong with them, where they hurt and such."

"Not at all," the doctor replied. "It's that very fact that makes them the ideal patients."

NO LAMB OR LION

Gusty March, such bluster.
And then again such balmy days of respite
Between storms; such lulls that it seems
Spring has already come, then sleet
Or snow or worse. Such a month, this March,
Never knowing whether it is lamb or lion,
Or what to do lest spring catch it unawares,
Lest the flowers come too soon,
Lest the blossoms are caught out
And returning cold nips them in a freeze.
Is March a villain setting snares
For precocious blossoms?
Or is it so unstable in its moods
That it can only be depended on
To be undependable?

BATTLESHIP IN THE WOODS

Coming out from Wilmington, visitors get their first glimpse of her as they cross the bridge towards Southport-not all of her, but the masts of her showing incongruously through cypress trees.

A battleship in the woods: the U. S. S. North Carolina miles from the ocean and years from the war she was built to fight, a shrine now and a tourist lure.

Signs point the way to her inland mooring, and when visitors reach her they can look from her decks or from the big parking lot beside her into downtown Wilmington across the river.

The USS North Carolina was one of the last of the Navy's armored queens and with the USS Missouri, the USS Iowa, the USS New Jersey and the USS Wisconsin, one of the last five and mightiest to fire their guns in battle. Their era ended with the change in naval tactics from big surface fleets to aircraft carriers, missile launchers and fleets of missile-firing, nuclear-powered submarines.

A few still lie in mothball storage, awaiting final decisions as to their fates. Too expensive to operate for casual duties and too large and specialized for easy conversion, they seem likely to go, as the others have gone, either into scrap or to the states whose names they bear as memorials.

North Carolinians donated more than $330,000 in a statewide campaign to bring the USS North Carolina home. She was brought from Bayonne, N. J. in October, 1961, under tow and negotiated into a tight berth dredged as an arm off the Cape Fear River. There she sits now, and there North Carolinians expect she will sit permanently.

More than 2,000,000 people have seen her since she came. They have walked her decks, climbed her ladders, explored her turrets and sat where her captains and admirals have sat, on her bridge and in her control rooms, and they have not tired of coming. The crowds not only are as large as ever, they seem to be getting larger, and the commission which has charge of her keeps adding features or opening sections which had been closed. Various below-deck areas have been opened, allowing visitors to tour a complete gallery and cafeteria, bakery, butcher shop, grocery and staples supply, ship's post office and soda shop, engine room, medical and dental offices, and a shipboard museum, which contains among its treasures a magnificent silver service.

There was a time when fighting men on a fighting ship, eating in the USS North Carolina's messes consumed 15 tons of potatoes, 100,000 dozen eggs, 128,000 pounds of flour and 21,000 pounds of lard, as part of their rations in a normal 60 days at sea.

Now children sit in the captain's chair, and crank the handles of the anti-aircraft gun mounts, and pretend the things that seamen did on battleships and, except in pretense, in the woods, where the North Carolina rests at the end of all her voyages, never will be done again.

April 1967

WHEN SPRING COMES

White is the color of dogwood,
And pink when the root is split,
And purple's the wealth of richness
By which spring is welcomed in thrift.
And pink and purple, yellow and green,
These are April's blazon,
For April is the month that brings
Spring with all its beauty
And paints the lawn with daffodils
And a fragile range of blossoms,
When birds call greetings to each dawn,
And it sends us out in showers,
And lifts our spirits with a song
As lilting as its sunshine.

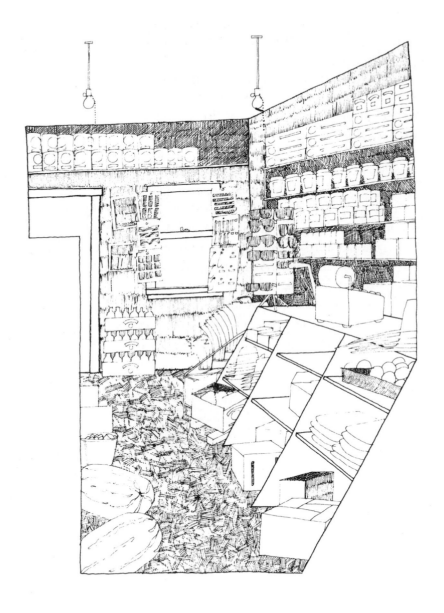

C BEN JONES
HE WANTS TO SEE YOU

You've read again and again about old fashion country stores. Ben Jones' place is the country store today. Types like him are as familiar at the crossroads of North Carolina as the filling station emporiums they operate. Most such businesses are well-kept and well-managed. Ben's customers like his just the way it is.

You expected things like it from Ben Jones. He was one for jokes and such, and if his people hadn't already had a mortgage on that Eastern North Carolina farm he grew up on they probably would have sent him to college. He had a way with books as he had with jokes.

He had a head on him and he was smart enough to realize while he was still a boy that farming and raising tobacco were becoming more and more tortuous ways to earn a living. As soon as he could find another way he took it.

He did it the summer after he left school. I'm going to work for old man Adams, he announced one day. There're too many mouths to feed on one tobacco crop, and I'm the hungry kind. So he did what he said he would do and by the time he was called in the Draft in 1942 he was as good at old man Adams' business, which was running a store and filling station at the crossroads, as the old man himself.

He was more filled out when he came back from the Army and more certain about things. He still was one for joking, though, and he had become a talker who could make people want to listen. There was something else, too. He had managed to save most of his Army pay and he got the terminal leave pay soldiers got then for being in the war, and he knew what he wanted to do with the money.

Old man Adams was showing his age by then, and Ben Jones made him a proposition. It worked out to Ben buying out the old man, some in cash and some to be paid out of future store profits.

About the first thing Ben did was to get new signs, and on the big one, set up on the roof you could see it coming either way, he had the sign painter put: "C Ben Jones - He Wants To C U."

Everybody who knew Ben had to laugh, and people who didn't know him but saw the sign would laugh. And Ben laughed, seeing as he had suspected that a little fun was good for business.

What's the C for, they'd ask him. For Cash, Ben would say. Cash is what it takes to keep you going and credit is what puts you in the hole.

Everybody would laugh at that too. But they kept wanting to know what the C was really for; he'd always been Ben or Benjamin. Where did he get the C? From Cyrus, he would tell them sometimes: my ma called me that for the man who was an inventor. Or Cicero, he would say another time; the preacher had my folks call me that because it sounded impressive. And nobody knew which if either version was true.

The store he had under the sign was like any you see around the crossroads across the state. It was out from town, close enough to be handy and far enough out so the competition didn't hurt it. There were, as there usually are at such stores, gas pumps out front, and gasoline signs and racks for motor oil and tires. On one side there was an old grease pit. On the other there were used and broken down appliances like electric stoves and washing machines and a collection of old 60-gallon drums and old crates.

Out behind you could see a hog pen and a shed which usually had in it a pig or cow or calf Ben had taken in trade or bought to butcher. Scattered all around were soft drink bottles, empty motor oil cans, junk and boxes.

It didn't look like Ben was running a beauty project or, when you compared the place to places in town, much of a business either.

But up there, on the roof, over it all, was the sign:

C Ben Jones — He Wants to CU.

Inside Ben had everything in as big a muddle as out. There was rat poison for sale on a rack on one side of the cash register and headache powders on the other. There were candy bars in one part of a glass showcase and soap and socks in another part. There was a wooden bucket of salted fish on the floor and a couple of salt-lick blocks for livestock beside it. There were overalls, oatmeal, cheese, hams, shoes, bridles, an ice cream box, canned goods, a meat counter, electric ranges and appliances, prunes, a soft drink box, and gloves and baby bottles and patent medicines, all stirred up together, sitting here, hanging there, or on top of one another as though all had been brought inside in a hurry and never put away.

The customers were mostly country folks. They'd come early in the morning as if to get primed for work. Sometimes, they'd come back around noon for a bottle of pop and a pack of crackers or cup cakes. In the evenings they'd come back to sit.

As time wore on a different kind began coming. They'd pop in businesslike for a loaf of bread or a carton of milk, or the fixings for a quick lunch, and perhaps gasoline for their lawn mowers. They were the new kind in rural North Carolina, the kind who live out of the towns and have jobs in them.

Saturdays were Ben's busy days. A lot of the business

17

places in the towns and cities had taken to closing Saturday afternoons, and places like Ben's got the trade. Folks in rural sections, still liked to go to the store, to sit if not always to shop, Saturday afternoons and evenings. Sundays were slow, with most customers just hanging around for want of a better place to kill time, and now and then a car would stop to get gas, or pop or candy or bread.

Weekdays, Saturdays, Sundays, mornings and nights, Ben was always there. Often the customers knew so well where in the muddle to find things they'd wait on themselves. So the hours were not too wearing on Ben, but he was always there, leaning over the counter, or wrapping up an order of fatback at the meat counter, or standing by the cash register, talking and joking.

If somebody came in and wanted a horse collar for a mule, Ben had it, maybe hanging hidden by some raincoats or plant bed cloth, but there. If somebody wanted a freezer, Ben had it or would get it. If it was liver or if it was beans, it was there. And as his business grew, Ben invested the profits in farmland, becoming as busy a farming operator as a merchant.

For as long as Ben had lived in the county, the roads that made the crossroads at his place had run past farms and tobacco fields, and mules had been in the barns, and pigs in the hog pens near each of the barns on each of the farms, with a scrawny cow or two in the pastures.

The tobacco fields were mostly gone now, along with a lot of the people who had tended them. Houses with carports and picture windows had taken the land, and the people instead of working on the land were working in towns or as far off as Raleigh in businesses and offices.

And Ben grew older and stouter, and the sign faded and was repainted, to fade and be painted again. Each time with the same words:

C Ben Jones — He wants to CU.

The C didn't stand strictly for Cash anymore but for Credit, too. By now Ben had most of his customers on the books. When they'd buy something, he'd take a ledger out from under the counter and write down the purchase on a different page under each customer's name.

The roads changed, the farms gave way more and more to houses for people working away from the land. Ben grew fatter and his business did too, and some of those who came in regularly began to realize they'd heard some of his jokes before.

In the town down the road, as in some other small towns in North Carolina, merchants were finding their old customers dwindling and the new ones taking to shopping in Raleigh, or the nearest big town. The old firms along main street began to fade away. The big general store on main street was turned into a place for storage. The movie theater had closed at four or five years back, and the dry goods store had nothing behind its locked doors but dust and counters to show what it had been. The competition of the big stores in the cities, and the changing ways that carried people to cities to buy, had hurt. Even the businesses that had survived the depression were losing to the roving wheels of the automobile.

But Ben's business grew, as it has grown at many stores like his out from the towns at the many crossroads of rural North Carolina. When suburbia took the farm lands, Ben's place and the places like it were there to catch the trade, supplying in the off hours and the days the city stores would close the loaf of bread or pound of weiners that had been forgotten, or the bottle of pop or package of cake mix you might buy on an impulse.

By now the sign on the top of the place was so familiar, Ben very seldom was asked about the C. Anyhow, the business on the books became so much more the rule than cash that the joke Ben used to make wouldn't hold.

They were sitting around in the place, as they always did on Saturdays, with Ben talking and joking by the cash register, when this fellow came in. He looked like he was selling something. But he wasn't, he told Ben; he was just looking around.

Help yourself, Ben told him, and then, laughing, went into a story about how a stranger once had come looking and had asked for the wrong thing at a country store. It was one of Ben's jokes, that story of the stranger, and by the time he'd finished telling it Ben and everybody in the place, this fellow and the bench warmers, was laughing.

Couldn't help noticing your sign, the fellow said. What's the C stand for?

Ben thought a minute and began as if he was going to tell his joke about Cash and Credit. Then suddenly he stopped.

Not for anything, he said. Just some foolishness. I just had it put on there for foolishness, sort of to make a slogan. Fact is my name has an F in it: Benjamin F. for Franklin Jones.

Maybe you were right and didn't know it, the fellow said. That C could stand for a lot of things about C, from what I can see, and this place of yours. Things like C for *casual* and for *commerce* at the *crossroads,* and maybe for *continuity* because tied up here is what used to be with what is and what things are coming to. And, looking around, at the clutter, he grinned and said, and maybe also for *confusion.*

But looking at you, I'd say more likely it's a C for *contentment.* You have found your place in a C for the *changing* world about you and you are C for *content* to let things go as they will.

Some of the bench warmers weren't sure whether to laugh or wonder. But the fellow laughed and kind of nervously they all began laughing too.

It was kind of a joke on the crossroads' biggest joker.

And Ben, because he was smart enough to know when he'd been topped, laughed as if he'd made the joke himself.

ALL THE STORY ISN'T IN THE TEXT

Many of us, when we were growing up, were admonished to never write in books. We were told any marginal notes and comments we might be tempted to jot down on the pages defaced books and might distract or irritate other readers.

But many people who should know better ignore the old admonitions. Books in public libraries as a result tell not only the stories their authors intended to tell but become annotated with gratuitous observations, criticisms and, often indecipherable bon mots.

Mostly the errant annotations deal with errors made by the author or the printer. When the author carelessly describes the same character as red-haired on page 6 and bald on page 38, one of these anonymous reader-cum-editors who mark library books will write on the margin on page 38: "See page 6. Let's get our facts straight."

Or if a harmless word misspelled becomes a dirty one, you can expect to find someone has underscored it and written in the margin: "At last a spark of life," which is to let you know this particular reader-editor is as blase as he is sharp-eyed.

And when the suspense is building up and you're racing through the words to picture in your mind what it is the author is trying to convey, suddenly the spell is broken for you by a ball-point notation: "Ha. For real kicks read 'Lady Chatterley.' "

You can try to ignore the notations but you'll probably find, unless you are unusually strong-willed, that they catch your eye. Despite yourself, you'll wonder what prompted somebody to write two big exclamation marks beside what to you is a very prosaic paragraph. You'll puzzle over the reason for the question marks where you can find no cause for question and wonder if you've missed the point because you can't guess why a word was underscored.

Sometimes the annotations are scholarly. Written in pencil across the bottom of the page, you'll find the subject of the biography you're reading once taught history at Davidson or was in his youth a bicycle mechanic in New Bern.

Such would-be contributions to knowledge are wide-ranging. A mention of a pie in the text of a novel may prompt a volunteer annotator to give the basic recipe on the margin. A reference to some prominent person or historical personality may inspire the comment: "He was 69 when he died," or "his father never married," or "Josephus Daniels wrote about him. There never was a bigger crook."

Then there are the kill-joys. They're the ones who let you know on page 69 in the mystery novel you're beginning to enjoy that they've already deducted who the murderer is or point out in the final chapters, where the hero-detective is closing in on his suspect, how what is written there doesn't mesh with what was written five chapters earlier.

Finally there are those who, too late, annotate the annotations.

One of those wrote in a larger scrawl beneath the annotation of an anonymous nit-picker:

"If you're so smart, why don't you write a book yourself."

CAUTION: POETRY AT WORK

The driver trapped at the barricade sees only the inconvenience of it.

A turning bulldozer blocks the left lane, a gang of men with shovels block the right, and the driver waits and fumes.

The inconvenience is for his convenience later in wider paving and better shoulders but later doesn't serve him now. The scrapers moving in ordered herds, snorting smoke, with diesels straining, and the big sheep's foot packers make pictures for photographers but not for him.

The yellow-painted sawhorses used to mark the danger areas, stretching ahead of him like hurdles for a relay race, make a picture in geometric design, spaced along the paving block after block. The driver has no patience for perspective or for art; they're yellow obstacles to him.

At night when the flares are lit, a necklace of light winds up the hill ahead. There's poetry in the scene, but not for the man hurrying to beat the car coming from his rear that in a moment will cut him off.

The men strung out with picks digging around the drain basins and for the culverts at the driveways might look, to a man who had time to look, like figures from some artist's conception of the machine age version of the Man with the Hoe. The signalman with the red flag could be a symbol if a man had time to ponder him. The driver in the morning rush and hunting a hole to pass in the panic race home has no time for imagery.

The barricades will go eventually; the new paving already is being laid. The bulldozers, the workmen, the scrapers and sheep's foot packers will move on to other jobs and the flares will go.

24

They make a picture and there's poetry in the light and sounds.

But the driver has no time, and in time the imagery will be swept away, forgotten in racing mob using four lanes then where there were two and seeing nothing except the hole opening in the relentless traffic.

1963

THE MAN WHO KNEW HEMINGWAY

It hadn't occurred to him that his having known Hemingway was particularly exciting. It had been so long ago and, after all, he had known people as interesting.

But when he mentioned Hemingway — casually in recalling how he once had driven a jeep from a landing strip to take Hemingway into Cherbourg — one of them gasped in surprise. "Hemingway!" she exclaimed. "Ernest Hemingway!"

Yes, it had been the famous Ernest, the author of so many short stories and novels and so many reams of war correspondence, the Ernest that students now study about in contemporary literature.

But the Hemingway he had known was not the prestigious celebrity but a quiet, big man with a beard who spoke quietly and somewhat falteringly and had asked him to take a detour deep into the combat zone to buy some cheese. He had wondered at the time, with the sound of artillery thundering in the distance, how Hemingway could expect to find the village where he would get the cheese. Yet, Hemingway seemed to take it for granted that, now in the midst of a war, the men he wanted to see about the cheese would be alive and still selling cheese.

And when they got to the village Hemingway who spoke French fluently asked about the cheese-selling friend. Though Hemingway could not have been there since before the long war had started, he was recognized and French people came out of houses in the village and greeted him as though he were their liberator. And Hemingway found his man and got his cheese. There were several boxes of it and it smelled rank.

Another time he sat in a town from which the Germans had just been driven by American troops and listened as Hemingway and a few friends talked and drank. There was Bob Capa, Life photographer who called Hemingway "Papa" and who later in another war was to die in French Indochina. There was Bill Graffis, a captain who often traveled with Capa, and there was a bird colonel who supplied the drinks.

Capa was a quick talker with what sounded like a Hungarian accent, and he could tell a story well. So could Graffis. He had been an advertising man and he had a flare for conversation. The colonel, too, was something of a raconteur. Only Hemingway, the writer of so many words, the author of so much well-read conversational prose, seemed to struggle to put his words together. He was diffident and, as he spoke, hesitant, as if he were carefully choosing each word he used.

It all was so long ago that he could not remember now any of the stories nor even well the men. But it came back to him now, as they urged him to tell them more of Hemingway, how the war had brought so many like Hemingway to their crest in life and how "Papa" Hemingway, bearded and diffident, had in the war been a man in his element and at the same time a paradox.

THE CHARACTER OF WRITING

The fledgling author trying his wings with a first novel decides, now that the first draft is finished, that a few preflight adjustments must be made if his fiction is to fly.

He oils it in a bath of James Jones profanity, advances the spark with a John O'Hara seduction, steams it in a stream of consciousness after Proust, decorates it with a coating of Hemingway philosophy and instruments the whole according to Faulkner.

And when the manuscript finally lands before the publisher it reads like nearly all the fiction which these days flies in such bewildering coveys across the literary landscape.

What he had fashioned is not a literary creation but a composite rendering of borrowed concepts. The author's original ideas and inspiration have become so lost in the supposed necessities of salability that about all that remains of his own are the names he gave his characters.

He has applied the first rule of authorship: You must read before you begin to write. But he has missed the message: To write well you must read wisely. Once the message is understood, you will recognize the essential quality of the good novel lies not in the style nor even plot but in the integrity of the people who live in it.

If the people can be made real to the reader, if they can be identified with people whom the reader knows or may be made to believe do exist, if they react as people would react in real life, then style becomes only a matter of technique and the plot merely a means of demonstrating they are human.

Balzac proved that in his classic "Cousin Bette." Prolific

as he was, the talented Frenchman was not the best of writers — others excelled him in style and plotting — but he had a way of making his characters immortal.

Flaubert demonstrated it in his endurable "Madame Bovary." The result was a character so memorable, involved in circumstances so intriguing that both she and the circumstances have been recast again and again by later authors for every generation through the present.

That principle more than sex, profanity or philosophy was the power of Hemingway and Faulkner too. Their characters are people, even when they are nameless, as the convict in "Old Man" by Faulkner and the fisherman in the better-promoted (if no better written) "Old Man and the Sea" by Hemingway. Sex, profanity, philosophy and style were not the end goals of their craftmanship; rather these were means to an end, serving their purposes by demonstrating the humanity of the character and by demonstrating also that a man must be what he is. Such was the convict and the fisherman; they could not escape even when pressing on patently was pointless.

The character may be a Holden Caulfield, as in J. D. Salinger's "The Catcher in the Rye," struggling only to escape from himself, or a Mick Kelly finding herself, as in Carson McCuller's "The Heart Is a Lonely Hunter."

In no case need he be a hero; in some novels he appears as a "non-hero." But he must exist.

In Albert Camus' symbolic novel "The Plague" the symbolism carries its point all the more persuasively because it is expressed in the lives of people who in a quarantined Oran, in their weaknesses and strengths, are symbols of ourselves. And in Reynold's Price's "A Long and Happy Life" Rosacoke Mustian is as identifiable to her Eastern North Carolina setting as the Warren County pecan tree in which she first found her Wesley Beavers.

But again it should be understood identity is not the essence. There have been many good novels in which the key character stood behind the scenes as the narrator or appeared as a disguised image of the author.

Style counts of course, and plot does too. But style is the embellishment even as it also may be the strength of the story, and plot the circumstances by which the characters are revealed.

In Thomas Wolfe, style was his glory – and sometimes also his curse. Yet the rhetorical poetry which flows in such great meandering rivers through his prose might never have flowed in print, or long ago might have ceased to flow for readers, if it were not for the character of Wolfe himself, either as Eugene Gantt or George Josiah Webber, to give the torrents meaning.

No novel worth the name can be constructed by formula. To recognize the importance of characterization is merely to admit the immensity of the novelist's challenge.

He not only must understand human nature so well that he is both fascinated and disgusted by it; he also must have the rare and super-human capacity to convey life and understanding.

That is the enigma in the message to be read from the works of writers who survived their first novel.

And therein may lie the frustrations of the aspiring writer and his publisher to produce literature an easier way.

And therein may live the reasons so many of the novels printed are dead before the hapless characters in them can be buried.

1963

THE TRUTH OF FICTION

Literature is an art but there are many who, living by it, teaching it or sitting in judgment on it as critics and reviewers, feel driven to define its intangibles. And even as academic authorities on Wolfe periodically attempt to explain the inexplicable quality of his style, some of us would reduce the alchemy of writing to a single basis element.

Can that really be done? Is there any one quality which more than others distinguishes good fiction from the mediocre. Or, to put it in more basic terms, is there any feature which counts more than all others in the writing of a novel which publishers and readers will accept?

In a previous article on the subject, it was suggested that the essential and distinguishing quality is characterization. Now, three able practitioners of the literary art accept an invitation to speak, each briefly and to the point.

Reynolds Price, Tar Heel native, author of the Sir Walter Award novel "A Long and Happy Life," and a member of the English Department faculty at State College:

"The surest way to write bad — because dishonest — fiction is to begin considering what publishers or readers 'want.'

"Good fiction results when human feelings of great intensity are understood by a writer who can communicate those feelings, that intensity, that understanding through the instrument of beautiful — because truthful — form."

Lodwick Hartley, head of the English Department at State College, an author himself and a seasoned and able literary critic:

"With the major contention I certainly agree. The ability

31

to create living characters is the greatest gift of the writer of fiction.

"I do not think, however, that the analysis of what the tyro does is valid.

"It may be true that he imitates; but more often, I fear, he does so unconsciously rather than consciously. . . What the contemporary novelists mainly lack is commitment."

Jessie Rehder of Chapel Hill, a member of the English Department faculty at the University of North Carolina and a teacher of creative writing who, in the opinion of at least several of Chapel Hill's creative writers, is one of the best qualified of North Carolina's literary personalities:

"I agree (with what the article set out as its major premises). . . I think fiction is a matter of of making a character. It is a matter for the writer of corralling the facts, and as Joyce Cary added, not only the facts but the feeling behind the facts.

"You have a bad style maybe. Dreiser did. You have frothy people maybe. Fitzgerald did. You have only one thing to say: since life makes no sense, all you can do is learn how to face what is going to be your fate. This last is what Hemingway had to say.

"You can be so infatuated with words, so much so that you almost drown in them. Wolfe did. You can be so infatuated with them that in the end you get lost in them. Joyce did in "Finnegan's Wake."

"But all of these people made characters and made other people — readers — care about the characters. That's all you can do. All any writer can do. You can, as Hemingway once said, make something through your invention that is not a representation but a whole new thing truer than something true and alive, and . . . if you make it well enough, you give it immortality.

"But the immortality comes through the characters,

what they do, what they feel, and what comes out of what they do. From Ahab, Huck Finn, Daisy Miller and Stephen Dedalus to Seymour Glass and to the characters who are being born this minute in the invention of young writers, it is *the people* who make the book."

1963

THIS LAND IS YOUR LAND

Woodrow Wilson Guthrie was a folk singer who sang with the voice of America. He once was called "a national possession, like Yellowstone or Yosemite" and he wrote hundreds of folk songs, each with a message of hope for the common man.

"I am out to sing songs that will prove to you," he once said, "that this is your world and that if it has hit you pretty hard and knocked you for a dozen loops... no matter what color, what size you are, how you are built, I am out to sing the songs that make you take pride in yourself and in your work... "

During the days when Woody was wandering and singing, one of the hopes of the people was electricity for farms and rural homes. About 1941, he was hired by the Bonneville Power Administration to write some songs about Grand Coulee and Bonneville dams.

"I pulled my shoes on and walked out of every one of those Pacific Northwest mountain towns," he said, "drawing pictures in my mind and listening to poems and songs and words faster to come and dance in my ears that I could ever get them wrote down."

In some 30 days, he wrote 26 songs for Bonneville. "They played them over the loud speakers at meetings to sell bonds to carry the high lines from the dams to the little towns," Woody once recalled. "The private power dams hated to see these two babies born to stand up out there across those rock-wall canyons, and they tried every trick possible to hold up the deal." In the end, though, he added, "our side won out on top."

One of the songs he wrote about those great dams was

"Roll On Columbia, Roll On." Guthrie's message of hope is typified in a line from the chorus: "Your power is turning darkness to dawn."

Last year, Secretary of Interior Stewart Udall presented Guthrie with an award on behalf of the U. S. Government for his life-long effort to make the American people "aware of their heritage and the land." Udall described Guthrie as a "poet of the American landscape."

Woody Guthrie couldn't attend the ceremony. He had been stricken 15 years ago by a rare muscular disease and by last year he was bed ridden and paralyzed. On Oct. 3 of this year he died, leaving behind him a legacy that is spelled out in his most famous song:

"This land is your land, this land is my land,
From California to the New York island,
From the redwood forest
to the gulf-stream waters,
This land was made for you and me."

December 1967

(Adapted from a "Conversation Piece" by Dick Pence in the "Rural Electric Newsletter.")

35

A KING IN EVERY FAMILY TREE

Ancestor worship didn't die when Mao Tse-tung purged old China; it still flourishes in these United States, rampantly in the South, persistently in New England.

Almost none of us, it sometimes seems, can resist the temptation to swing occasionally from our family tree or, lacking a suitable one, invent one to match our aspirations. Either way, we can do so confident that since all of us are the children of Adam, we all can claim we are nobly descended. And if we can afford the price of our vanity, we all can find somebody who will sell us a coat of arms.

Lest modesty deny you your birthright, consider the mathematics of probability. No matter how low your present social status, the odds are that somewhere in your background there was a castle and perhaps a King. And lest your pride swells too greatly, the odds equally favor in your ancestry both rogues and roues.

To understand the probabilities, begin with the ancestors you know. Everybody has two parents. Working back from there, even if you aren't certain of their names, you can count four grandparents, and eight great grandparents. If you carry your calculations back still farther, the total of ancestors over a span of say 64 generations would be virtually beyond counting.

If you take one generation as the equivalent of 20 years, 64 generations would equal 1,280 years. Thus in approximately 13 of the 20 centuries since the Nativity, we all have inherited some of the nobility and some of the villany of 18,446,744,073,709,551,615 people.

That fantastic figure is cited in reference books as the classic **example** of the difficulties of accurately and honestly tracing a family's genealogy. Large as it is, it has not discouraged either the hundreds of us who every year retain genealogists to trace ours, nor the thousands of us who, skipping the genealogists, claim a common heritage with a name that happens to be the same as, or similar to, our own.

Actually, the same ancestor appears several times in the family trees of everybody, which reduces the total number of ancestors but still leaves the total fantastically large.

Actually, too, none of us can know all our ancestors back more than a few generations. Even in 10 generations, we have had 1,024 ancestors apiece. In that number there would be as many we would not care to boast of as there would of those we would proudly acclaim.

So whether your name happens to be Washington or Arnold, or Grant or Lee, remember before you brag that you carry the genes of traitors as well as patriots. Think upon that while you reflect upon your heraldry, and consider that the least of those with whom you deal may, by the odds of genealogy, be nobler than you.

THE FLIM-FLAM MAN'S MOLESKIN BONANZA

The Flim-Flam Man, Mordecai Jones, and his sidekick Curley Treadaway set the country chuckling in a movie based on Guy Owen's novel, *The Ballad of the Flim-Flam Man*. A sequel, *The Flim-Flam Man and the Apprentice Grifter*, related their further adventures in the mythical Cape Fear Country. As Curley tells us in the following story, the Flim-Flam Man is still living up to his name.

By Guy Owen

It all started like this: Mordecai Jones and I were tooling along in the Carolina low country when we ran up on a delivery truck turned over in a drainage ditch. It was August and naturally hotter than the bottom clinkers of hell. So everlasting hot the Flim-Flam man wasn't in much of a mood to do business. Every now and then we'd stop off at some one-gallus spot in the road and plant a crooked punchboard or try for an order of something out of his scarred-up satchel, even just a Bible or maybe a year's subscription to *Grit*. It was piddling business for such a master of chicanery, and I figgered he was doing it just to keep his hand in, so to speak.

Of course, he perked up when we rounded this curve and spotted the truck half-turned on its side near this old tar-papered tobacco barn. It seemed like Providence sending us a fresh mark.

"Why, it's like manna falling from heaven in the Good Book," my pardner says, rubbing his hands together.

I pulled in behind the wreck and we both hustled out. I saw there wasn't much damage, except maybe to the driver's pride. He was laying a cussing on somebody for hogging him off the road, a hairy-armed, tattooed fellow in sweaty khakies and a canvas hunting cap.

The truck wasn't damaged much, but there was one big carton that was pitched out in the clay ditch. It was bigger than a coffin and busted at one end, so these trap-like things had leaked through, some of them bent, shiny as new steel traps.

I saw the old chisler's oyster eyes skimming over that busted carton. Directly he says, "How much will you take for those mole traps?"

"Mr. Jones," I blurt, "don't do it." What in the name of sin would he do with all those mole catchers? I'd wager there weren't that many moles in all of Cape Fear County.

"Let me handle this, Curley," he says.

The tattooed driver took off his cap, scratching at his bald spot, all the time canting his eyes at my pardner. "What you want with all them mole traps, old timer?"

I'd be interested to know myself, but I think to myself: That's for him to know and you to find out, Buster.

Mr. Jones allowed he was raising a garden and the moles were becoming an intolerable nuisance. "There's nothing I despise more than a blind pestiferous rodent like that." His eyes seemed to snap and on his high forehead this vein commenced throbbing and you'd 've thought his mama had been scared by such a varment when she was carrying him.

The truck driver drawls, "I'll let you have the whole shooting match for ten dollars, I reckon." As it transpired, there were 500 traps in the carton.

Mr. Jones counters, "I'll give you five."

"Sold."

I said, "Shoot-fire and save matches," too low to be heard, as Mr. Jones peeled off a crisp new five spot. I figgered he'd overreached himself for once. I guess the driver did, too, for he was sniggering to himself while he helped me load up the box of shiny mole catchers.

Anyhow, Mr. Jones promised the truck man we'd send back a wrecker, while I slid in and cranked up our disguised hearse and eased back out on the highway. We had just painted it a nice shade of blue with GOSPEL WAGON wrote on both sides.

I should've swallowed my spit and kept quiet, but I couldn't help busting out, "Mighty thoughty of you taking that load off his hands thataway. You bought yourself a white elephant, if I ever saw one."

"Remember the Good Book, Curley. It says help your neighbor get his ox out of the ditch." That was one of his sayings.

"It don't say you have to make asses of yourself in the process, does it?"

"Just hold your horses, lad."

"But, Mr. Jones, you can't get shed of 500 mole traps in a month of Sundays. I can't even remember the last time I saw a blame mole." I waved out the window at the big tobacco farms with brick houses and all. Even the martins had clorox bottles for nests instead of old-timey gourds. "Why, these farmers are so prosperous nowadays they don't half of 'em tend a garden, not one of ten even pretends to keep a cow." I told him we'd have better luck selling ice boxes to Eskimoes or maybe our gold-leafed Bibles in a whorehouse.

But Mr. Jones never budged an inch, just clamped his jaw firm as a pump's mouth. He allowed it was a shame the way farmers had abandoned the land and gone citified, but, then, it just gave them more leisure to hunt and trap. "I don't see why some of them shouldn't be put to hunting and trapping moles."

"Hunt and trap, my foot." Farmers was one tribe I

40

knew more about than he did, since I was raised so far back in the sticks they used foxes for yard dogs and owls for roosters. I still didn't get the drift of his new scheme, let alone the *modus oporandi*, as he called it.

But Mordecai Jones seemed set up and a lot more chipper. His lean face took on color and didn't look so much like last year's hornet's nest. He said if he could see the Golden Gate Bridge and the concession stand at the Daytona Speedway, he guessed he could palm off a few measley traps and turn a tidy profit at the same time.

"It'll be as easy as shooting shad in a barrel, son. All we got to do is apply sound business principles. All we need to do now is to create a market for those goods we just invested in." He allowed that was the principle that was running the whole country. "Or maybe I should say ruining it."

All this time he was poking around in his beat-up valise, pushing things aside — money belts, punchboards, shaved dice, and the like — until he uncovered a mess of printed handbills I'd never laid eyes on before. He fished the roll out, smiling a yard wide, unrolling the newsprint on his bony knees. "This ought to do for our bait, Curley." I saw he had some newspaper clippings to act as a clincher.

"Well, I'll be a son of a side-winding sapsucker!" I didn't slow up but I could read off the big print at the top: "$5.00 offered for uncured mole skins." His handbills said that a new scientific breakthrough had made mole hides even more desirable than mink or chinchillas, and the clippings claimed that moleskin coats were all the rage in New York City and sold for two thousand dollars a piece.

"Take a gander at that, my boy."

Mr. Jones showed me a newspaper picture of a half-naked model wearing a dyed moleskin coat that didn't hardly come down to her navel. She was skinny as a rail, but had on a proud smile, like she was tickled pink to be wearing mole hides.

"What do you think?"

"Mr. Jones," I say, "that durn coat is like a barbwire fence. It protects the property but it sure don't obstruct the view."

That one's so old it's got whiskers on it, but the old chiseler chuckled over it and seemed to enjoy it, so I forgot about being aggravated at him for buying the load of mole traps.

He was folding up the handbills, sort of shaking his head. "There's no accounting for taste — especially where spoiled city women are concerned." And he winked one eye a tad.

We stopped at the first garage we came to and sent back a wrecker to haul in the turned-over truck. And we hadn't gone more than fifteen miles before we came to a tobacco market town on the Cape Fear River. All you could see from a distance was a silver water tank, sawmill smoke stack and a three-story white brick hotel. But when we crossed the muddy Cape Fear on this rusty bridge, the little town didn't look so blistered and down-at-the-heels. You could tell the tobacco warehouses were open and the August auctions had commenced. There were knots of farmers on the sidewalks with golden hanks under their arms, big trucks of flue-cured tobacco lined up before the tin-roofed, sky-lighted warehouses. There was something else, too, if you knew how to scent it: the smell of money in the air.

The Flim-Flam man must've caught a whiff of it, craning his long neck and sort of popping his knuckles. "A likely looking metropolis my boy. Something tells me this is prime mole-working territory."

We checked in the hotel and grabbed a bite and had a

good rest. Then while I went around town and tacked up the handbills that offered five dollars per mole hide, Mr. Jones cased the three hardware stores in town. It turned out the moleskin caper worked sort of like the punchboard trick, where my pardner sold the crooked boards to store owners and I happened along afterwards and punched out all the big winners.

Next morning the old grafter sallied out and I've never seen him look so perky and full of ginger. He was dressed up in a new white suit with his pearly Stetson at a jaunty angle, the chain of his gold watch dangling just so, a flower in the lapel of his coat. He was spruced up just like a Mr. Gotrocks, with a linen handkerchief in his pocket and two-toned perforated wing-tipped shoes, polished so you could see your reflection in them. There was even this flashy diamond on his little finger to match the pin in his yellow and lavender tie.

Like he predicted, it was easy as snitching pennies from a Sunday school collection. Naturally, I couldn't go in the store and be seen with my pardner, but I was close enough to the door to take in most of his spiel. And didn't he make a grand rigamarole out of it though? Of course, the hardware dealer had already got wind of the big mole skin bonanza. All Mordecai Jones had to do was make out like he was the New York buyer, setting up a regular route, out signing contracts to buy the mole hides. He flashed a few coarse notes and pulled out a legal-looking contract. In no time he had the apple signed on the dotted line.

"I know it sounds ridiculous, Cap'n Ware, but you and me can't be held liable for the decadent taste of New York's women."

"Moleskin coats," the old codger cackled. "What'll they think of next, I wonder?" But he said he'd deal in frog hides if that's what the city fools craved.

43

"My sentiments precisely, sir." Mordecai claimed the whole thing was symbolic of the search for novelty amongst rich city slickers.

But he allowed he thought this was one fad that might backfire on the high mucketymucks. "It's my feeling those coats won't wear too well, new scientific treatment or no."

"Well, that's their little red wagon, eh, Mr. Longfellow?" He acted like he was right happy at putting one over on the New York furriers.

After Mr. Jones had finished his moon pie and Dr. Pepper, he folded his copy of the contract and left, saying he'd be back in three weeks to pick up his first delivery of mole hides.

As he waltzed out, he tipped me a wink. I waited just long enough for the hardware man to wait on his customers. Then I went in toting a sample of my new model mole trap with a patented spring and safety catch. I'll admit I'm no salesman — but I didn't need to be. Before you could say Jack Robinson, I'd sold 100 traps at two bills a throw. It seemed an enduring shame.

We made three more stops in Cape Fear County, and everything went off without a hitch. Then we were clean out of rodent traps, so we made ourselves right scarce.

But I still think every now and again about those mole skins gathering dust. Come to think of it, I guess they'd commence to smell pretty tipe after so long a time.

Later, Mr. Jones said, "I guess those fellows killed so many moles in Cape Fear County they must have upset the balance of nature."

It could be. We never stayed around to inquire. Like the hardware man said, "That's their little red wagon."

(Guy Owen, poet, folklorist and author, is a member of the English faculty at North Carolina State University.)

WHO SAID MAN WOULD NEVER FLY?

So many people are traveling abroad and flying nowadays that I feel I must tell about my most memorable trip, if only to establish I too have had my fling.

This trip of mine happened during World War II. I had flown into Holland on an airborne operation and had written stories about paratroop and glider infantry attacking the Germans around Eindhoven and Nijmegen. It had been an impressive if unsuccessful demonstration of British and American airborne power and now I had flown back for follow-up coverage.

The story this time was to be about retrieving gliders from the battlefield so that, presumably, they could be used on another front.

Hundreds of gliders were scattered about the neat flat fields in the Eindhoven-Nijmegen area. Many had been destroyed or damaged by enemy fire or had crashed with their cargoes of men and equipment. But quite a number had survived and those not stripped by scavengers for wheels and instruments had been sorted out for pick-up.

The pick-up system involved rigging a loop at the end of a tow rope connected with the glider between two uprights. One of the old C47 transports used in those days by the U.S. Troop Carrier Command then would fly low over the pick-up position trailing a cable with a hook. When things went right, the hook would catch in the tow rope's loop and jerk the glider into the air. The system was chancy. Although it had been tested before, it was still experimental.

My mission was to ride in the first of the gliders to be retrieved and, barring misadventure, write what happened.

The glider pilot with whom I was to fly was a stranger. But I haven't forgotten him. The pilot and I braced as the tow plane roared over us. We were slapped against the backs of our seats when the hook caught and the glider took off.

Not long after we were airborne and had straightened out to head south, we ran into rain.

We'd been up perhaps half an hour when the pilot punched me and swung the control wheel over to my side of the cockpit.

"Try it for a while," he yelled.

I swallowed hard and took the wheel, not because I wanted to but because obviously somebody had to steer. I had flown several times before in both British and American gliders as a passenger. I had a vague idea of what had to be done but I never before had tried doing it.

Through occasional breaks in the clouds and rain I could see the earth far below. Well, we can't get lost, I rationalized, because we can go only where the tow plane pulls us.

After we had been in the air for what seemed to me like most of a day, the pilot yelled something and pointed downward. I could see a large greenhouse below. I had no idea where we were. I could imagine crashing into all that glass.

The pilot yelled again. I thought I heard him say, "Get ready to go down." I was sure I must have been mistaken because I couldn't believe he'd take a chance on my attempting a landing.

I shook my head and yelled back. "No. No. You're the pilot."

The pilot grinned. "Chicken," he yelled. He pulled the wheel back to his side, spotted a landing strip and cut loose from the tow rope.

We immediately lost speed. He banked the glider and circled. We came down finally with a couple of bounces and jolts. I got a ride from the airstrip, eventually reached Paris and collected my wits to write the epoch.

I didn't write how it felt to fly a glider. That was something that at the moment I couldn't put into words. I just wrote briefly that a glider which had flown against the Germans had been recovered to fly again. So much was happening in war news at the time I doubt anybody cared.

AN EASTER HYMN FOR A NEW DECADE

He is risen.
And as Easter comes this March of 1970
The world again rejoices
His victory over death.
And we rejoice
And our faith is renewed.
For in the Miracle of the Tomb
All mankind is renewed.
And no miracle in our science.
Even in feats beyond the moon,
Will ever so change our destiny
As did the first day at the sepulcher.
Now in this spring of a new decade,
Let us rededicate our lives
In the memory of His sacrifice,
To rolling away the stones
From the sepulchers of our time
So that we may in our lives
Rise to greater realizations,
Rise like the jonquil through the cold earth
Above the cold selfishness.
The encrusting self-righteousness,
Out of the tomb of self-interest
And know this Easter
"He is risen"
As our emancipation.

IT'S FOR YOU, MOTHER,
THIS IS MOTHER'S DAY

Don't cry for what is lost.

Plant something there to fill its place, as you might late beans when the early vine had died. . . or another flower where the first was crushed.

My father often told us that, she said. Sitting there, seeing it all and hearing it as in her father's time, she was all of them like herself who keep alive the century past. And now in 1967 she lived again somewhere back of 1880, or beyond even that.

Yes, that was the way Father would talk, she said. It was good that he could, So many couldn't you know. You can't imagine how it was.

Oh, so many were killed and some came home as good as dead. But my father, he'd been through it and had lost like all the rest, but he said dwelling on it wouldn't bring it back.

She sat in her rocker, with the small brown paper bag of pecans she would give as she always did to the great grandchildren when they came; almost unreal so white did she look, with skin nearly transparent and the veins standing high on her wrinkled wrists.

"But, Mother," they told her, "This is MOTHER'S DAY."

"Your day," they said loudly. And when she seemed not to hear they repeated it more loudly still: "MOTHER'S DAY, HAPPY MOTHER'S DAY."

"Yes, yes," she said hearing at last. "And you're all grandmothers."

"And I'm a great grandmother. Oh, Father, this would have made his heart glad."

"Yes, Mother, yes," they shouted, knowing that they must shout if she was to hear, "but this is Mother's Day. It's for YOU. We've come to see You. And the children are here."

And she smiled vaguely, her mind wondering years back, thinking perhaps how Father would have taken all of this.

It was strange how strongly her voice came when she had something she wanted to say, some anecdote from the past she wanted to recall, or some story as now on Mother's Day of Father.

"Half the time," one of them said, "you barely can hear her. I don't think she has seen a thing yet that we've brought."

And they sat smiling at her, waiting until she would.

* * *

You couldn't have known, the old doctor said, how primitive American medicine was just those few decades ago.

Why in my own time, in the early years of my practice, and, of course, I've been retired now for several years, motherhood was the great gamble of a woman's life.

Now you think about it. I'm sure you've read about it. You don't have to be a medical man to know. Many women died in childbirth, many of them, and the statistics of stillbirth and the deaths of infants and mothers too, of course, were beyond anything you could believe nowadays.

Oh, being a mother was not for weaklings. It's a good thing, he said, with a smile playing across his old man's face and in the wrinkles about his old man's eyes. It's a good thing women are the mothers. The males aren't man enough for it.

I've been called out many a night halfway across a county in a buggy, racing to the bedside. And when I'd get

51

there, the husband would be in such a shock that the neighbor who'd come to fetch me would have to lay him out on a couch and give him spirits. And the mother — well, many a time the baby would have come by the time I'd get there — she'd be smiling, with the baby beside her.

I've heard many of them say, I tried to tell my husband, Doctor, there wasn't any cause to bother you.

But in so many other cases, oh so many tragic cases, I'd be too late. Many times it wouldn't have mattered if I'd been there. There would have been nothing any doctor, now or then, could do.

* * *

The bronze is green now, but the beauty of it remains, depicting and memorializing the most important soldier in all man's wars. She sits, this mother, on this monument "To the North Carolina Women of the Confederacy," with a book, perhaps a Bible, open on her lap, On her right, a son kneels holding a sword that might have been his father's.

The foliage there on Capitol Square, where the tableau is placed to look out on Morgan Street, frames the monument with a special beauty these spring days. And the green of the leaf, and the hedge and the bush and the well-groomed grounds, give it a background, and blend in a season's harmony with the green-strained bronze.

And it is, as some see in passing it, appropriate. For this is the picture of Motherhood and the message of Mother's Day: The eternal bringing forth, the ever green and the promising, the new bloom where one had died, the new seed for one that failed. This is the tradition of tenderness and yet strength, as old as all mothers, and as new in hope as all of man's tomorrows.

MOTHER'S DAY

Two roses bloom in May.
Two roses on an old bush,
Two roses and three buds.
It was started as a cutting
Taken from an older bush which
Her father's mother had grown.
She had cherished it
For its old-fashioned beauty,
The deep red beauty of its large
Red roses, and he loved it
For his mother's sake.
And when his daughter married
He cut from it a part and rooted it
And gave it to her for her yard.
Now it grows there in deep red
    beauty,
Bearing its roses each year in
    May,
Bearing now two roses and three
    buds,
For Mother's Day.

SWEET MAMA

She had been "Sweet Mama" to them since the oldest of them had first begun to talk, and she had instilled in them, as she had in their mother, a sense of home, family and North Carolina. Her story is a Mother's Day story not only for those whose family memories go back to the North Carolina of yesterday but also for those of younger years who wonder how it was when mother's mother lived.

Lying in the hospital bed, taking oxygen under the transparent tent, she looked paler and more fragile than any of them could remember.

She lay motionless and silent. Now and then she would open her eyes. She seemed unaware they were in the room with her.

"She doesn't know anybody," they whispered. "She'd say something if she did."

And she lay there unknowing, neither seeing nor hearing as far as they could tell, while they stood unsure whether to leave her or stay.

When she was born, more than 90 years ago in Warren County, no one then living could have foreseen oxygen tents or intravenous fluids. Nobody could have foretold she or anyone else of her day would lie wasting and unaware in a hospital. In her day, you were born at home, you gave birth at home, you were sick at home, and when the end came, unless it came by war or accident, you died at home.

In her day, home was the beginning, the center and the ending of North Carolina life, and Warren County and the other eastern counties where *homeplace* was a word with meaning were bound in vines of kinships. North Carolina was not merely a political division; it was also a family. If you were a Jones, you need not explain your antecedents; everybody knew them. There might be strangers, perhaps when people met away from home, or ran into one another on trips to the county seat or once in a while to Raleigh, but if they stopped to talk long enough they would discover they were cousins.

When somebody like William Polk or Gerald Johnson wrote a book, or a Smith or a Parker did well or poorly, or Judge Kerr's boy went into politics, cousins they might not have heard of shared their glories and commiserated in their miseries.

You weren't Lucy Jones or Henry Wilson. You were Franklin Jones' daughter or so and so's grandchild or the nephew of Lawyer Wilson.

Now she lay there, a frail and silent relic of her yesterdays, under sedatives, a white-haired shadow of herself, covered over like her great grandchildren's Easter baskets under the cellophane-like transparency of the oxygen tent.

She was nearly as far and as long from home as she ever had been. In all of her more than 90 years she seldom had been more than a day's journey or a night's rest away. And when she was, she usually was with somebody in her family or those who had known her so well and so long they were as close as relatives.

War had taken her son's father. Their jobs had too. But they had returned. In the pattern so true to her North Carolina, neither sons nor daughters went so far or stayed so long that she did not see them often.

True to her North Carolina and her generation, she could recall the times when people on holidays went to the mineral springs and carefully, self-consciously explained the waters were good for their health. The war for her was not

55

those wars fought across oceans; it was the war when the Yankees came and about which and in which her father or grandfather did this or said that and Cousin Mary's mother hid the silver and had the house servants take the horses into the woods.

They watched her, and they stood by the door of her hospital room and along the walls.

"The nurse said," one of them told the others, "that she knew who she was last night."

And another said quietly expanding the nervous, whispered conversation, "She took some water in a spoon."

It's remarkable, they agreed, how she has managed to stay on. They could not bring themselves to say what they really meant. Their tongues revolted at the cold word death.

For more than 90 years she was in the North Carolina family of interminable cousins, uncles and common memories as much a part and a symbol as the Confederate statue in the courthouse yard and the dogwood blossoms in the spring.

So many of those she had known already were gone, and so also were the life and the ways and the North Carolina of her generation.

Now she lay there unaware of both this and them. Her daughters and sons, her granddaughters who had called her "Sweet Mama" since the oldest of them had first begun to talk, her cousins, they all either were there or had been there or were waiting to come.

It was as if all that tied the old North Carolina to the new and the past of everything to the restless present waited there with her.

Back at the homeplace, her great grandchildren played, knowing only that "Sweet Mama" was sick and that their parents and grandparents seemed more than usually concerned.

And one generation lay weary but not knowing it, and two generations waited by the bedside, whispering and wondering, and a new generation played until its time would come.

And for a moment in time, time stood still, letting the old linger and the young vaguely imagine how their years would be.

THAT ALL MAY KNOW

May fills the promise April makes
And brings a promise of her own,
Blessing all new growing things,
Blessing fresh growth in the old.
May crowns the beauty spring began,
Adding more in flowering delight,
Showing crops and gardens how to grow.
And May has the voice of birds,
Singing as birds do on such days,
Singing in a chorus of sweet sounds
An anthem in which all Nature joins
That we may know that we are blessed,
That we may know the wonders
That He works.

LIKE A FAITH RENEWED

How does June come?
As a child happily to the end of school, June comes.
As growing crops take root,
As skies turning bluer, and like the lengthening days.
like the fragrant grass,
Like the first of summer's warmth comforting the earth,
June comes.
June comes as a bride and also with assurance,
Without simpering but with poise,
Like nature's music, softly.
Like the young child laughing, June comes.
Like a prayer, with sincerity and hope.
Like a hymn for all that God has created;
Like a sermon spoken in the tongues of souls;
Like a faith renewed,
June comes.

THUS DOES A GARDEN GROW

So you weren't going to have a garden this year. Well, what are you doing with that hoe? Admit it, you couldn't break the habit. Admit it, even if things did get out of hand. There's noting to match the growing urge that grips a backyard gardener when the growing season comes, and if you planted a lot more than the wife can use, you can always try to give it away.

Hurry, hurry, hurry. That's you, the wife said. You should have known it was too soon to set out those tomato plants.

She was right, he admitted. He'd lost most of three batches already this spring trying to plant before the weather settled.

The last blow had fallen in the frigid kiss of an unexpected light, late frost, and it had been so dry. This wasn't his year. Well, he'd said he wasn't going to have a garden. The few tomatoes had been a last minute weakening to the old spring urge.

Now another chilly morning. The light summer suit was another of his premature decisions. People hurrying past him as he walked from his parking lot to the office were shivering. No more tomato plants. The wire grass soon would cover the place he'd set out the others.

Of course, a couple of hills wouldn't hurt. She couldn't object to that, and maybe a few cabbages.

On the way back to the parking lot at lunchtime, he saw the garden supply store ahead. A display of tomato plants, hearty in individual containers, stood in the store's doorway. The plants were as big as his would have been if they'd lived. A few like that, he thought, and he'd never know in a few weeks that he'd had a setback with the others. With luck, they'd be blossoming shortly.

He stopped and studied them. They were good plants.

What's the price? he asked through the doorway. How many? the clerk asked. Would you sell as few as a half dozen? he asked the clerk. Sell you one or all you want, any way you want them, the clerk said. Good plants. Wilt-proof.

A dozen? Yes, he said, make it a dozen. I usually put out at least four dozen but I'm cutting down this year. The clerk picked up a box. Got some mighty healthy cabbage plants, the clerk said. Well, he said. I guess I better pass on the cabbage. Where are they? The clerk showed him. They were healthy looking.

Well, since I'm here and I'll be putting out the tomatoes a few cabbages won't hurt. Make it a dozen cabbages, too, I guess.

Seems to me I remember you coming by last year for some bell peppers, the clerk said. Got some good ones. You could take a dozen. Shouldn't have any trouble finding a place for a dozen. No, he thought, a dozen peppers didn't sound like over-doing it. Make it a dozen, he told the clerk.

He set the plants outside, around the corner of the house, when he got home. He felt like a conspirator.

After lunch he got the shovel, saying nothing to his wife. While she cleared away the dishes, he worked in the garden spot in the backyard digging hills. When he came to the house to get the plants, she came to the door and shook her head, looking at him and saying nothing.

By the time he had set out half the tomatoes she was outside.

Where are you going to put the corn rows? she asked half smiling. And the butter beans and the pole beans?

She was kidding him, he realized, and he kept digging and planting as though he were lost in his thoughts.

She shook her head and watched. Then she began handing him the plants to set in the hills. He grinned.

Corn rows? he thought. It was getting a little late and he had to get back to the office. Well, he wouldn't over do it. When he had washed off and had started to the car, she called to him.

Please, she said. No corn. We still have a freezer full from the other years, and it's filled with butter beans and snaps, too. . . please.

It seemed warmer by the time he reached downtown. Warmer weather was on the way. A few days of sunshine and those plants would be on their way. After he'd parked, he found himself walking again along the route by the garden store. There was another way. He should have taken it, not that he intended to stop. No point in over-doing a thing.

Corn, well, she'd brought it up. Wonder how late would be too late to set out a few hills. Corn. Butter beans. Snaps. Please, she'd said. He looked at his watch. If he was quick about it he could stop at the store and ask how late he could put out a little, that is, if he was going to. If he was quick it wouldn't take any time to ask. But he'd have to hurry.

Hurry, hurry, hurry; that's you, she'd said, and it was only this morning. Hurry, hurry, hurry. How late would be too late just to try?

May 1965

THE VIEW FROM THE NINTH FLOOR

By J.C. Brown, Jr.

The trees have grown a pale green, camouflaging Raleigh's slums which lie to the south and east. Beyond the city auditorium, three blocks away, six lanes of highways undulate through the spring to the deeper green horizon. The spring day, and the highway that puts the beach only three hours away, make it difficult to think of work. But this afternoon, the traffic isn't moving. Six abreast, trucks and cars are backed up beyond Shaw University, blocked by a multitude of black bodies. Police, some armed with what appear to be shotguns, move back and forth across Wilmington Street. After a time, a company of the National Guard moves to the flank of the blockade. A mist suddenly hides the protestors, and they begin to move quickly toward the Shaw campus – all but a group of about five or six, and finally they too yield to the tear gas or whatever it was. The traffic moves again. For how long, nobody knows. Most people feel that tonight will be worse than last night. On Fayetteville Street, people cluster. There is a restless aimless movement on the sidewalks and an embarrassment. There are no jokes about Negroes as 200 black marchers move past the Sir Walter carrying taunting signs of protest against the white man and wearing looks of hatred. There is no fear in these faces. There is an unmistakable dare.

Martin Luther King was murdered last night, and Raleigh – a city where most officials and citizens have held dear the belief that "our Negroes are contented" – had demonstrations that erupted into riots.

I don't think the destruction and the ominous gatherings

on the street are so much acts of vengeance for Dr. King's murder as expressions of frustration. For several years, and especially for the past several weeks, Raleigh's Negro poor have been trying to tell their city something about their needs as they relate to city hall. Nobody listens, or if they do, nobody acts, the Negroes feel. There isn't much evidence that Raleigh has really made a serious effort to understand what the problems are; you just can't see them from a ninth floor office window. Nobody but a Negro really knows what it's like to be black, always; and so we can only guess what Dr. King's death meant. To some Negroes it certainly meant that King's non-violence doctrine was a foolish failure. To others, his martrydom was a Christian victory. I think to the Negroes who led the protests, who broke the windows, and set the fires, Dr. King's death epitomizes how they view the white man's attitude toward the Negro. That is, we don't view him as a man. When he acts like a man, when he objects too annoyingly, we kill him figuratively and literally. The protests could be the Negro's way of saying, "I am a man. I'm going to make you know I exist, feel pain, and can act." If he feels he's laughed at, or ignored when he goes through peaceful channels, it's not illogical for him to assert himself violently.

I don't have any answers, but communities which are viewing their Negro population from ninth floor windows might at least make sure they really know what's going on down there, and make an honest attempt to understand what the Negro is saying. It isn't much fun to live in fear, and there is fear in Raleigh today. Offices are closing early, school closed earlier, the children are frightened, the Ice Capades are cancelled, and rumor is the curfew has been advanced to 5 p.m. The sky at 4:20 is black, and it has started to rain, which is the brightest hope for a peaceful night.   May 1968

A FATHER'S PRAYER

FATHER, I thank you that I have become a father too. Help me to remember that I, too, was once a child.

Give me patience: That I may give my sons and daughters time to learn for themselves, as all children must, what cannot be put off for later.

Give me forebearance: That I may always find the time to tell them what it is I must say. And let me always tell them out of love.

Give me understanding: That I may know something of what my children nurse within their hearts. And let my heart be full for them.

Give me restraint: That I may never let anger dictate how I act and speak to them. But neither let me vacillate or fail to say what should be said.

Give me judgment: That I may judge wisely their acts and actions — both what they have done and what they have not done — and measure their doings by the same scale as my own.

Give me insight: That I may see not only their faults but their strengths. Yet let me learn not to see things that will correct themselves.

Give me humor: That I may laugh with them and know they should sometimes laugh at me.

Give me sympathy, and compassion, too: That I may share their sorrows and, in sharing, help them learn to accept what must be.

Help me ever to provide well for them. Yet help them to know that all they want may not be theirs to have.

Instill within me a sense of values such that I may help them wisely build their own.

Give me humility along with strength that they shall have these, too.

And help me, Father, in my faith to You to be as a child such as was your Son, that I may guide my children in His footsteps and walk in them myself.

AT THE OCEAN'S EDGE

If you would know the coast of North Carolina, you must drive the length of it, along all the miles of twisting roads, across the bridges and the ferries and through its many towns.

You must see it at its uppermost end, at Knotts Island and at Coinjock. You must come in from Pt. Harbor to Kill Devil Hills and at another time from Mann's Harbor. You must stay a while along the way and see it with time enough to reflect upon it, at Nags Head and Manteo, and drive along it down the Outer Banks to Hatteras, and see the lighthouse, and go to the end of the road.

You must take it in slowly, sipping rather than gulping, not as if you had to drink the ocean in a single swallow.

The long and level stretch of highway leading past the hotels, restaurants, inns and summer houses along the Nags Head ocean front — that is a sip to savor. The long drive south, through Stumpy Point, Englehard, Lake Landing, New Holland, Belhaven and on down the road, through Washington and New Bern to Morehead City, that is an adventure to take in pleasure. And you must go to Ocracoke and to Portsmouth Island and put in a weekend at Cedar Island and at a place like New Topsail Beach. Spend a night here and a day there, stopping, taking a different impression at each place and drinking in the sights along with long miles until you stop again.

And you must see all the towns whose names dot the map along the inverse curve from Cape Lookout, out from Harkers Island, to Smith Island, at the mouth of the Cape Fear.

They are names with magic in them and stories too.

Along the long strand, from the Virginia line to South Carolina, history lives among the dunes and tangles, and cottages rise and inlanders play on vacation not far from where battles were fought and the Lost Colonists vanished with the enigma of the Croatans.

Much of it is still nearly as it was, but change is coming, eating into it as the ocean eats into the Banks. And the old beach hotels, to which people once came from Wilmington by trolley car and to which as at other points along the coast, nearly the same clientele came year after year, are changing. Some already have gone and others will, and there'll be new, big motor hotels such as you find along the major tourist routes. But there still is time.

The beach is a place where many things are buried in the sand — old hulls of lost ships and shells, and children's sand buckets and people sleeping with only their heads showing. Here along the coast, people come to bury their troubles in the sand, and to wash away the things that become part of living inland.

You relax here, on the beach and along the coast of North Carolina, and you take a vacation from your world.

When people used to come to the coast, they'd come as they did to the mineral springs, staying for at least a week because there were no easy ways to travel. They usually would eat where they stayed, and some of them never went into the water. They came for the health — not the frolic. Leisure had to have a purpose then. It wasn't as now when fun needs no justification.

But it's still there, the spirit of it spilling over it like the restless surf across the sand, building here and removing there, burying and washing up. Here, along the coast of North Carolina, in the beach season, change is eternal. And the magic of the attraction if it is as constant, as imperturbable to change as the yearning that now brings us again to the ocean's edge.   August 1967

70

A PIG FOR FATHER'S DAY

Sunday will be Father's Day, and a lot of fathers who all the rest of the year live out of step in this permissive age will enjoy then a respite of respectability.

There'll be gifts and greetings and maybe the children will come home and maybe the preacher will say something appropriate to the observance in his sermon. But Father's Day in too many homes is father's only day, and the cards and gifts he receives are more gestures than tributes.

If you read the books some psychologists are writing, if you follow developments in the Revolt of the Young and compare the status of the father of yesterday with the father of today, you might conclude fathers have gone out of fashion.

Don't be misled. Young people have been challenging parental authority throughout history. The young have always been in revolt. Every generation has perplexed its elders.

We say to fathers, hold steady. Fathers are here to stay. Fathers must remember that. And mothers, sons and daughters must accept it.

Various experts have said something must be done to upgrade the Father Image. Bosh. If there's anything wrong with the Father Image, it's that the Image has become more important than the Man.

What we fathers need to do, Dad, is be ourselves.

Forget the Image and the theories. Stop playing a role; be your own man.

Don't become so preoccupied with winning the family's acceptance that you lose yourself. Don't become so bent on molding your offspring according to the mores of your generation that you become a symbol of the past at the expense of being a person of the present.

Do the things that come naturally. Dress the way you like, eat the way you like, live the way you like. In most families nowadays everybody else but father does. Why should father be different?

And don't be different in your treatment of and attitudes towards your children than you are in relationships with other people. You've learned to get along with business associates and friends, employees and employers. the same principles apply to sons and daughter. Kids are people too. All of which gets back to the point: Be natural, be yourself.

We knew a father when we were young who had seven children, a mongrel dog named Reason and a pet pig named Susie. The dog would trot behind the family car when the family went to town and get in fights with the town dogs. And the man would boast that Susie the pig was smarter than people, and she'd follow him everywhere, even into the house at times.

The children were embarrassed. They were ashamed to be part of a menage that was also a menagerie, with a mongrel dog running escort and a pig that thought she was a person.

So far as we know, all seven of those children today are leading normal, reasonably happy adult lives. Perhaps the embarrassment of a childhood with a Reason and a Susie gave them the incentive to achieve respectability.

We don't have a pig, but maybe we should.

Maybe if all of us who are fathers would stop worrying about what the family thinks of what we as fathers do and have and would be ourselves, we'd be happier men and the fathers of happier families.

RAIN BEFORE DAWN

The rain came while I slept,
Before dawn, awakening me,
Crashing, unrelenting,
Beating against the windows;
Beating, blowing, rushing down
    the drains,
Storming across the roof,
    mercilessly,
In a thunder of noise.
The rain came, shattering the
    night,
And when the time came
At last for day to break,
The rain still fell
With a fury on the house,
And the dawn was only a pale
luminescence,
And the house was silent
As if afraid.

PIGEONS ALL OVER

Pigeons all over the place, that's the trouble. Pigeons and pigeon litter on the sidewalks, pigeons on the roofs, pigeons on Capitol Square and on the statues, and on the still pristine ledges of the new State House.

If they were good for something, these dirty birds, except for taking peanuts from children and stealing from the squirrels, it might be different.

Once it was different, and Dale Starbuck, Jr. of 2304 Fairview Road remembers it well. Once Raleigh's pigeons were for eating. Pigeons still are but not so generally or with such gusto as then in Raleigh, when pigeon coops were nearly as numerous as pigeons and starlings are now.

"When I was a boy 48 years ago," Starbuck recalled, you used to see them out on St. Mary's Street before it was paved and in East Raleigh.

"They looked like miniature houses stuck up on poles."

Some of them, the pigeon coops on poles, were kept painted and had colored roofs. Some were merely enough of a shelter high enough from the ground to give the pigeons shelter safe from cats.

They'd have little holes in them like windows and doors so the pigeons could get in and nest. The people who had the little houses on poles in their yards would let the pigeons lay eggs there. Then they'd either hatch out the eggs themselves or let the pigeons hatch them. When the little pigeons came, they'd sell them for squabs.

"They were tender like partridges or quail," Starbuck said, "and they were served on toast. They sold for about 25 cents a squab."

Some eating places around town back then specialized in

74

them. The old Giersch's restaurant on Fayetteville Street was one that did.

"They were mighty good," Starbuck recalled a bit wistfully.

Probably a mighty good remedy for the pigeon problem, too, if anybody now dared try it.

July 1967

CENTER OF THE YEAR

Who needs a calendar to know
    July?
Not country folk when leaves curl
    in the heat,
Nor townfolk sweltering on
    hot streets.
Who has to tell what July brings?
Not patriots taking time off for
    the Fourth;
Not one who knows his summer
    skies,
Or watches summer lightning flash.
And surely not barefoot children.
And when the sun burns lawns
    and fields,
And makes the beach sand hot
    between bare toes,
And the air is strangely fresh
    after storms,
Who cannot say this is the month
In the center of the year?

IF YOU WILL LISTEN

If you will listen on Capitol Square, you can hear North Carolina speaking, you will hear it murmuring through the shrubbery and trees. If you will look on Capitol Square, you can read the story of North Carolina from the monuments and plaques.

In the cool corridors of the handsome granite Capitol, you can follow the footprints of history, and you can stand in the rotunda below the old copper-clad dome and see beyond the circular railing with the polished brass trim the doors behind which laws were made for North Carolina through the years through 1961.

The lawmakers meet now in a new State House (which they call the Legislative Building) but it was of the Capitol that sculptor Gutzon Borglum once said: "There is no building in the country of its size which for color, for care in construction, and purity of style, is its superior."

In the original design for Raleigh, Capital (Union) Square was the center of the city. In North Carolina now it is the heart, a 6.2-acre historyland with carefully-kept green lawn, shrubs, flowers and more than 50 varieties of trees.

In the spring, the square is a floral exhibit, sharing its beauty with birds, squirrels and pigeons, bench-sitters, strollers and touring school children. Three types of camellias planted around the Capitol alternate blooming seasons with azaleas, tulips, roses and 30 varieties of shrubs.

The Legislature has gone to the State House but the Capitol still houses the Governor's office, the State Treasurer and the Secretary of State. The old House and Senate chambers are preserved, with their noisier pasts.

Outside, among the trees and shrubs, the statues and old guns and markers serve as reminders, too.

George Washington stands on a pedestal looking down Fayetteville Street, atop a circular mound just south of the Capitol's south entrance. The statue is a bronze copy of the original by Houdon in the Virginia Capitol at Richmond. It was placed in Raleigh in 1858 and is flanked, on each side of the iron fence around it, by a pair of French-cast cannons made in 1748, mounted at Edenton in 1778 and brought to Raleigh in 1903.

Charles Brantley Aycock, Wayne County native and North Carolina's 1901-05 Education Governor, stands to the west of Washington. The statue, by Borglum and erected in 1924, recalls Aycock's service in launching the present-day North Carolina public school system.

Zebulon Baird Vance of Buncombe, governor 1862-65, 1877-79 and U.S. Senator 1879-94, stands on the southeast portion of the square as a statue by Henry J. Ellicott erected in 1903.

At the southwest side, looking onto Morgan Street, is a monument by Augustus Lukeman honoring North Carolina Women of the Confederacy.

Ensign Worth Bagley, the first American officer killed in the Spanish-American War, stands as a statue by Packer on the west side of the square, to the southeast of the Confederate Monument, and a Spanish naval gun, set up in 1908, is, with the statue, a favorite gathering point for small boys.

On the east side, at the head of New Bern Avenue, an impressive monument by Charles Keck features the statues of three North Carolina-born Presidents — Andrew Jackson, James Knox Polk and Andrew Johnson. Jackson, a native of Union County, served as President from 1829 to 1837; Polk, a native of Mecklenburg, from 1845 to 1849, and Johnson, a native of Raleigh, from 1865 to 1869.

The Confederate Monument stands at the head of

78

Hillsborough Street. Its 75-foot granite shaft is surmounted and guarded by bronze Confederate soldiers. A 32-pounder cannon is mounted on each side of its base. They were cast in 1848 and were taken from the Norfolk Navy Yard when it was abandoned by the U. S. Government in 1861.

To the south of the monument to the Presidents, striking a pose in a statue by Ruckstuhl erected in 1911, stands Charles Duncan McIver (Moore County). He founded the State Normal and Industrial School which has become the University of North Carolina at Greensboro.

They tell a story of North Carolina, these statues and monuments on Capitol Square. You can read it if you look at the inscriptions and study the plaques. It's there in the green quiet of the lawn and the shading trees, and it lives on for North Carolina in the granite, marble, brass and copper of a building which for color, care of construction and purity has no equal.

THE APPLE TREES

In April, the apple trees,
survivors of an assortment
of fruit and pecan trees
planted when the house was new,
are covered with pink blossoms,
And I am glad
I let them stand.

But when the blossoms are gone
and apples form and fall,
worm-filled, bird-pecked, rotting,
and branches sag and grow downward,
creating a tangle
the mower cannot penetrate,
I forget their April beauty.

And only because April
seems to come sooner
for me each year,
do I suppress the summer impulse
to rid the yard of apple trees.

IF A FISH IS A GIFT, WHO
LOVES A CHEERFUL GIVER?

A weekend seafarer, a city man with a cottage on the coast, says fishing has taught him a lesson about land-lubbers.

The first rule for getting along with inland women, he says by way of explanation, is never to bring back fish unless you've had them cleaned.

It's a hard lesson to accept. Some fishermen refuse to accept it. But if they would, a lot more spots, flounders, blues and such would go into skillets than now go to cats or out the back door with the garbage.

It's a shame, but the fact is most of us, womenfolk and menfolk alike, are callously unmoved by fish and game that have to be dressed.

We may not look a gift horse in the mouth, but we're nearly all given to looking gift fish in the gills.

The distinction is important; there are relatively few gift horses given these days — except to women's colleges for income tax purposes, whereas gift spots are as plentiful as the returning fishermen who catch them.

Women, practical beings that they are, cover the situation with the implicit if not always stated observation that if the fish, the spots, were worth the keeping, they would be kept by the fishermen's wives.

The seafarer points our logically that he doesn't have a wife and even if he did, she couldn't be expected to keep and cook every fish he catches.

But why, he is challenged, do fishermen and hunters turn up at such inopportune times to be so generous?

Supper's all ready to serve, or the weekend's menu is set, the wives will argue, when in comes one of their husbands' cronies with a string of fish, or a carcass of deer, or a bag of dead ducks, expecting to be congratulated.

And even if you like fish and game, the wives will add, why be overly grateful for a catch of bone-filled fish which must be scaled and cleaned when you can buy fish, already-in-the-fillet for a fraction of what a man spends going fishing?

The erstwhile seafarer rests his case. He accepts the facts and acts accordingly.

No fish to give anybody, he says stoutly, unless they're ready to put into the pan. That's the way it has to be and he makes no bones about it.

The lessons of fishing, he expounds philosophically, are as bountiful of truth as the lessons of the ages.

As proof he cited the Scriptures:

"It is more blessed to give than to receive."

5-STRING BANJO

One Joe Sweeney of Virginia was credited with inventing in 1831 a little fifth string running from a little peg halfway up the neck. It was this version that became fantastically popular and was picked up by the country as a whole. It travelled west in the covered wagons, and one could be found hanging on the wall of any farmhouse or mining shack ... Today, the 5-string banjo is almost forgotten. Instrument companies produce very few. A Hock shop is the most likely place to find a good one. Still it is played by back-country people. Especially in the south. To accompany Ballads and play for square dances, and precisely because it is so excellently suited for such work, the old Five-stringer seems due for a comeback.

From: "How to Play the 5-String Banjo," by Peter Seegar.

All children acquire the belief that anything homemade is inferior to its manufactured counterpart. Light bread smeared with peanut butter and jelly is far superior in a school lunch to the ham biscuit and cold sweet potato. In the mountains before World War II, the magnetism of outside glamor had stronger pull than in most places.

Up until the '40s, many of my schoolmates had never been farther east than Asheville or farther west than Sylva. When you did travel outside the mountains, people would giggle and say, "So you're a hillbilly!" We were proud to be called mountaineers, but we did all we could to strip ourselves of the things associated with "hillbillies."

Nothing marked the hillbilly as much as his traveling habits and his music. People living in what we called, "way back in the mountains," had no roads worth mentioning

84

and they didn't especially need them, for they had no cars or trucks. They walked, whole families would faithfully walk 10 to 15 miles to town one Saturday a month, to see a movie or buy shoes and staples, or, just to come to town. The man of the household walked ahead, and a few respectful steps behind came his wife, and then a long line of children. When they reached the roads travelled by cars, they claimed a fair portion for their own, and they wouldn't deviate from their line of march just because the vehicle had a motor and horn.

Sometimes they brought their music to town with them. On Saturday afternoon, it was unusual not to find banjo players or guitarists performing in front of stores, on the courthouse lawn, and in the vacant lot used as a taxi stand. An old woman named, "Aunt Ida," who lived in town, would usually be around to do a buck dance if the tune called for it.

None of these people were beggars, although few of them ever had any cash money. Charitable instincts were accommodated by a blind guitarist with a tin cup who usually stuck around the front of the taverns, which specialized in 10 cent beer and fortified white wine.

Almost always, there would be a Yankee selling a spark-plug attachment alleged to cut down gasoline consumption and increase efficiency. He would have a gila monster to attract the crowd.

Ever so often, down from the mountains would come a delightful character named Foxy "Edderds" (mountain for Edwards), with hides to sell, or a unique performance to give, for a small price.

The most memorable of these never quite came off. He appeared on a street corner at the edge of the business section (after spending the morning drumming up an audience), with two cane-bottomed straight chairs, a fair-sized boulder, and a sledge hammer. He collected 10 cents from the few who had gathered, stretched himself between the chairs — head on one, foot on the other — had the boulder placed on his belly, and invited the strongest man in the crowd to break the boulder with the sledge hammer. There was fear in his eyes, for it was plain he'd never practiced this act. But he pled for someone to strike the blow. I was relieved when nobody would, but the artist was disgusted with his lily-livered audience, and stalked off mumbling angrily.

The musicians made no charge for their performances. They played because they felt like it, or perhaps because they had no money for the Saturday afternoon Western movie. The songs they played were ballads that had been handed down for generations, some brought by their ancestors from Britain.

We paid them little attention, and they paid no attention to us. The young townspeople of my generation professed to dislike the music. In our desire to prove our sophistication, we confused the folk ballads with the tasteless, synthetic tunes performed on radio by professional hicks, who added to our discomfort by their portrayal of the mountaineer. In the summer, there were square dances three nights a week, and we patronized these without embarrassment. They were popular with the tourists, so they had the stamp of sophisticated approval. And they were just too much fun to resist.

A summer Saturday in a mountain town, 20 years ago, had a carnival atmosphere about it, and must have had many of the appearances of an English fair of 200 years ago.

World War II, and still later, Governor Scott's roads program, reached back into the farthest mountains, and brought the mountaineers out. The folks who once came to town walking, now rode in new cars, and they went to the movies instead of playing their music in taxi-stand lots.

The town mountaineers formed civic music groups and brought in fourth-rate "classical" performers and ignored the rich musical traditions of their hills. I recall such a group threatened to sever its connection with the booking agency when one of America's most talented authentic folk singers, a zither player, was included in the season's offerings. Most of the audience went away grumbling that they'd heard their grandmothers sing the songs she sang and just as well!

The desire for imported culture reached into the back country, too. Women whose mother's sang of "Barbara Allen" and "George Collins" joined home demonstration choral groups and sang "Finlandia." Not many people, except in the most remote places, remembered the words to the old ballads; and not many people were interested in hearing them.

But a few remembered, and a few dedicated collectors combed the mountains to find them. A folk music performance came to consist of perhaps a banjo player on the steps of his cabin, playing and singing for one or two collectors with recording equipment. These collectors, as often as not, were neither scholars nor musicians. They simply had felt the excitement of discovering, on the lips of an old mountain woman, a song known to exist in Scotland 200 years ago, or been moved by the sorrowful story of a boy-gone-wrong on his way to the gallows tree. It was reason enough just to collect sorrows of life in pioneer America. As others collect old guns, paintings, and other documents of our past, they collect folk song, living documents of our people.

II.

One evening last month, if you were watching television, you might have seen a middle-aged, respectable-looking fellow named Frank Warner come out on the stage with a banjo, and play and sing a folk song called "Blue Mountain Lake," and chant a peanut vender's cry.

Everything about the production was authentic. Warner appeared bathed and shaved, and was dressed as Frank Warner usually dresses, conservatively, as befits a YMCA executive; the banjo he played was made by the late Nathan Hicks of Beech Mountain, N.C.; both songs were sung exactly as he'd collected them; the first from an Adirondack Mountain lumber jack; the second from a Suffolk, Va., peanut vender.

The next day, a syndicated newspaper tv critic wrote enthusiastically of Warner's performance. With unconcealed surprise, he reported that folk music is entertaining, exciting stuff performed in the unaffected manner of simple folk. Besides that, Warner is one heck of a good performer, and convincingly emulates the voices and inflections of the folk singers from whom he collected his songs.

The TV critic's surprise at finding authentic folk music entertaining is understandable. Folk song was never meant to hold an audience of millions, or sell a sponsor's product. The long-forgotten composers intended only to entertain themselves and their families, or strengthen their spirits against sorrow and hardship. Folk song was meant for kitchens, campfires, the cottonfield, the trail, and the stoops of pioneer cabins.

No matter the intentions of the folk who fashioned their ballads to fit the unassuming "noting" of a banjo or dulcimer, folk song has become much more than a diversion. Alan Lomax, in *Folk Songs, USA,* calls it a "truly democratic art, painting a portrait of the people, unmatched for honesty and validity in any other record... Folk song deals with realities — poor boys a long way from home, workers killed on the job, murderers..."

The fact that it was performed authentically on television is more surprising than the discovery that an honest performance is more entertaining than a synthetic one. Sponsors like to sell soap, or whatever it is they sell; and TV producers select performers who can guarantee them exposure to a large audience. Nowadays, the formula for success seems to require that the performers have highly-individualistic, frequently, preposterous styles. When they try folk music, the "folk" are lost in the performer's technique, which is calculated to focus attention on the artist with a three-day beard and a dirty shirt, open to the belt buckle. Folk music is often earthy, but it can't compete with a bare belly-button.

III.

Warner's performance, and a whole hour devoted to a program of authentic folk music, were especially satisfying to a North Carolina mountaineer named Frank Proffitt.

Proffitt is no different in background, education, and standard of living, from his neighbors in "Pick Britches Valley" in Watauga County. But Proffitt is set apart by his deep affection for the music, a memory that is better than common, and his skill as a banjo-maker. There is another quality, fragile and almost indefinable, but it appears in his letters and in his person.

My interest in Proffitt, the banjo, and folk music dates from the late winter, when a historian friend of mine wrote that a Frank Proffitt of Reese was making a banjo for use in a movie on Colonial music, being produced by Colonial Williamsburg, Inc. Lomax, who was Technical Consultant on the production, had recommended Proffitt upon the advice of Warner. My friend said that Proffitt, in his letters, sounded like a man who would be worth a story.

I was unable to find Reese on the official state highway map, but Rand-McNally located it in the northwestern corner of Watauga County, almost on the Tennessee line. It showed no road in an omission I later decided was for the preservation of wayward tourists unaccustomed to driving in the mountains.

I wrote to Proffitt, asking permission to visit, and quickly received a warm letter saying he "would be honored" to have me.

Proffitt writes in a small, legible hand, a mixture of printing and script, and he signs with his last name enclosed in parenthesis, which I took to be an invitation to be as formal or informal as I liked in my response. I was to come to know the hand and style well in the next few weeks, and like others who correspond with Proffitt, I place a high value on his letters.

His English has the ring of the mountains, which Dr. Cratis Williams of Appalachian State Teachers College at Boone, says is close to the manner of expression that generally prevailed in mid-19th century America.

Proffitt's tone is courteous and dignified, yet warm enough to invite the correspondence to continue. Like most mountaineers, he doesn't intrude, and this restraint extends to the proferring of information, gifts, or friendship. But given a sign, Proffitt supplies what you want precisely, and in good measure.

May 11 was cold and drizzly, and at breakfast in Boone, the waitress had aptly described the weather as "a dogwood storm." At Blue Ridge Electric Membership Corporation's Boone office, I got directions to Proffitt's home. Highway 421 to Vilas, turn left at the new bridge, cross the mountain, take a right onto an unpaved road at Bethel Church. The next day I learned from Cratis Williams that this was the pioneer route from Boone to Elizabethtown, Tenn. It's not an easy trip now, although the road is paved, and one wonders at the hardy pioneers who blazed the trail, and why.

Again, Williams supplied the explanation. In the decade preceding the Revolution, there were 600,000 Scotch-Irish in America. They found the good land of the coastal lowlands already taken, and so they migrated to the back country. These were the descendants of the Scots, Welch, and English, who had settled northern Ireland about the time Jamestown was settled. Their roots were in an old-fashioned area of England, which carried a wealth of oral tradition, and when they migrated, they brought their folklore with them.

Driving across the mountain from Vilas to Bethel Church (Reese is evidently just a postal address, for the natives will say you want to go to Bethel church, not Reese, if you inquire) is an unnerving experience. The easiest curves are hairpin ones. Many are more than 180 degrees, and in driving, you nose around them cautiously.

Alan Lomax wrote in *Folk Song, USA* that the banjo was given a fifth string by Joe Sweeney of North Carolina in 1840, and "it found its final home, after everyone else had grown tired of it, in the lonesome hollows of the Southern mountains."

91

There is disagreement about whether Sweeney was Virginian or Tar Heel, and exactly when he made his famous innovation. But there's little doubt that the fifth string gave America its only native musical instrument. While banjo-like instruments were played by primitive African and Egyptian tribes centuries ago, 19th century Englishmen referred to the five-stringer as "the American banjo," according to Grove's *Dictionary of Music and Musicians.*

It was actually the short-necked, fretted tenor banjo that flourished in the 1920's and finally disappeared into pawn shops and attics. The pioneer, non-fretted, five-stringer never lost favor among the people so closely identified with its sound: the Southern mountaineers.

There's a growing popular awareness of America's rich folk music performed by authentic folk musicians. Pete Seeger, author of *How to Play the Five-String Banjo,* writes that because the five-stringer is so excellently suited for accompanying ballads and square-dance tunes, it seems due for a comeback.

The five-string banjo travelled all over America, but you can hardly dig into its literature without getting back to North Carolina. Seeger's own banjo teachers included at least two Tar Heels, Bascom Lunsford and Samantha Bumgarner, and some other folk whose names have a familiar, native ring: Lilly Mae Ledford, Earl Scruggs, Rufus Crisp, and Uncle Dave Macon.

Seeger's book is in the folk music tradition of sharing. He states that he never got around to shelling out the four bucks neccessary to copyright it, and gives blanket permission for reprinting "whenever needed."

He dedicated the book to his teachers, "also to the men and women who, still earlier, taught them. But most of all to the folks who will learn from us, carrying an age-old tradition on."

When Colonial Williamsburg, Inc. embarked on a film production devoted to Colonial music, it hired Alan Lomax as technical consultant. Lomax's list of qualifications in the folk music field are too long to number; best known for his writing, he has also directed the folk music affairs of the Library of Congress and a couple of major record companies.

VI.

When Lomax needed an 18th century, gourd-type banjo, which antedates the five-stringer, he appealed to Frank Proffitt of Reese, N.C., a banjo-maker who had been recommended by Frank Warner of New York. Warner, who was reared and educated in North Carolina, appeared on the TV program, "Folk Sound, USA," and his authentic performances of folk song have done as much as anything to awaken the public to its musical heritage. Warner was the first performer to make a salable recording of the Tom Dooley song, which he collected from Proffitt.

It was through a historian at Colonial Williamsburg that I heard of Proffitt, and it was because of Proffitt that I found myself inching along a serpentine mountain road in northwestern Watauga County on a cold, misty, May 11th. The road, now paved, follows a route opened in the 18th century by Scotch-Irish pioneers who had found the rich coastal lands already taken. So they wandered mountainward, taking no treasure more comforting than their traditional music and folklore.

A short way up the mountain, an elderly mountaineer and a woman who appeared to be in her late 30's stood at the head of a dirt road leading to a house below. She carried a paper "poke." He pointed his thumb straight up, which was pretty much the direction of the highway. (It was the kind of land where one mountaineer told me, you had to be careful or you'd plow plumb through the other side.) He asked if I would give his daughter a ride to her home, a few miles away. As we drove off, he grinned and called, "Don't you two keep a-going on to Tennessee."

The woman explained that her mother was dead, and she had come over to clean house for her father and brothers. Both the flagging of the ride, and the dutiful daughter carrying her belongings in a sack, were common memories I had from my boyhood in the mountains, and it was easy to imagine that nothing had changed in the past 20 years. But it had. Mountaineers are well-traveled, now. Until recently, the woman had lived in Pennsylvania where her husband worked as a factory security policeman. Now he was working for the Highway Department down at Winston-Salem. He had left a car at home for her, but she couldn't drive.

The mountainside was still fall brown, washed with just the lightest shade of green, and dappled with the opening blossoms of dogwood, tulip trees, and fruit trees. We came over the top of the mountain, and spread before us was a lovely, long narrow valley. Through the mist that hugged the valley floor, you could see houses and barns here and there. Except for the buildings, it was the same sight that attracted the pioneers of 160 years ago.

My passenger got out in the valley, and I continued on a few miles to Bethel church, where I took a right onto an unpaved road that led into the country known as Pick Britches Valley or Mountain Dale. I asked directions at a dairy farm, and was told to keep going on up the mountain.

The road was narrow but easy to travel, and in a few minutes, I was at Proffitt's place. A steep hillside pasture came down to the road on the left. To the right, several feet below the road, was a swift creek, and, squeezed sideways between the road and the creek, was a garage supported partly on stilts. I parked on a short board driveway leading into the garage.

Proffitt's home lay across the creek and beyond 50 feet or so of lawn. It was a neat, fairly new 1½-story house, and looked more suburban than mountain. A hill rose sharply at the back of the house and levelled off into a small field, planted in strawberries.

A little boy in the yard ran into the house, and in a moment Proffitt came out to greet me. He was younger looking than I had expected, but everything else fitted the image created by his first letter; a tall and lean mountaineer, with a thoughtful expression, somewhat sorrowful, as befits a ballad singer.

My arrival coincided with that of the school-age Proffitt children. The oldest son, Oliver, was in Spain with the Air Force. The five at home were Ronald, 17, whose name was vaguely familiar; Franklin, 13, the best banjo picker among the children; Eddie, 10; Phyllis, 11, the best singer in the family; and Gerald, 4, who had greeted me.

It wasn't until I had returned to Raleigh, and resumed my correspondence with Proffitt, that I placed Ronald. He had entered an essay in our Silver Jubilee Scholarship Contest, and while it wasn't a winner, it was so beautifully and imaginatively written that we had reproduced portions of it and passed it around the office. Ronald, I learned, led his class at Bethel High School.

He comes by his way with words honestly; his father is a natural letter-writer. He's a man who sees a lot, knows what it means, and — happily — inherited a manner of expression ideally suited for communication. The speech of the mountains is a throw-back to the last century, according to Dr. Williams; and it has always seemed to me to be the richest and most useful of regional dialects. Such terms as "widder-woman" and "tooth-denist" and "soon of a morning" and "worse than common" (to state a condition of health) have more to commend them than their stripped-down versions. But it may be because I don't hear them much anymore.

In the Proffitt's living room, I learned that he is a farmer who follows the carpentry trade when there is work available. He had learned banjo-making from his father, Wiley Proffitt.

"They thought well of Dad's banjos." Proffitt said. Of his own work, he reported, "I don't make a great sight, but there's been a lot of inquiries lately – from up the country." Up the country meant New York, or most anywhere above the Mason-Dixon line.

"As they sell better, of course I become interested," Profitt grinned.

He gets $40 to $50 for what he describes as "a mountain man's banjo, but played by note, or the tune. Therefore, the fifth string is a very necessary part of this kind of playing.

"A mountain man will file the fret off of a store banjo in order to slide his finger up and down to play the melodies.

"I know nothing about banjo chords, but I can chord a guitar," he added.

It takes Proffitt about 30 days after receiving the order to deliver a banjo. This varies with the kind of wood requested, and the seasonal demands of the farm.

Frank Warner, who accompanied his performance on the television show, "Folk Sound, USA," with a banjo made by Proffitt's father-in-law, says of the Profitt banjo:

"He knows how to make the musical instruments in the old-time, painstaking way of his folks. His handmade banjo is not only a museum piece of authentic Americana; it is also a darn good 'ringing' instrument to be greatly prized by the best pickers."

The banjo made for Williamsburg is actually a *banjar,* or *banja,* a gourd-type four-stringed instrument. According to Grove's *Dictionary,* such an instrument was first described in English literature in *A Voyage to Jamaica,* written by Sir Hans Sloan, in 1688.

Proffitt pointed out that Thomas Jefferson, in his *Notes on Virginia,* written in 1781, mentioned the *banjar.* "The *banjar* was brought hither by the Negroes from Africa and was the original of the guitar," Jefferson wrote.

"Colored folks used to put coon hides on gourds and make banjars," Proffitt recalled. "As kids, we made them, too. Maybe with no head, just sound holes."

Actually, Proffitt made the Williamsburg *banjar* from sourwood, carved in the shape of a gourd and covered with a coon hide, a more substantial instrument than one made of a vine gourd.

Most of his orders are for the five-stringed American banjo. He makes them of maple, walnut, tamarack, oak, cherry, or other mountain woods. The heads are of squirrel, coon, or ground hog.

VII.

It was Proffitt's memory of mountain ballads, more than his wood craft, that endeared him to folk music collectors. Here is how Warner evaluates his contributions in folk music preservation:

"Frank Proffitt has a tremendous store-house of folk songs which he gained from his singing, playing, father and from other folks in his music-rich area. He has a very special understanding of his heritage and an unusual

97

appreciation of the old ways of his people."

Warner added, "I think people should be proud of their heritage — the ways of their folks — especially the rugged, hearty stock that came into our Carolina mountains and licked the wild ridges. Frank Proffitt is a proud mountain man, and I am proud to be his friend."

People who have discovered Frank Proffitt value the experience, and, as soon as you mention his name, will usually comment, with feeling, "A *remarkable* man," or, simply, "Quite a man." Dr. Amos Abrams, editor of *North Carolina Education,* relates that one of his fondest, most moving memories is of Proffitt receiving, unexpectedly, a gift from Abrams and Dr. Frank C. Brown.

Brown and Abrams, in 1938, found Proffitt, while collecting folklore which was later to appear in the seven-volume Brown Collection of *North Carolina Folklore,* published by Duke University Press. They collected many valuable songs from him. "You don't pay a folk singer, like $10 for 10 songs; but Proffitt had been so valuable, we wanted to do something for him, so we gave him a guitar. I'll always treasure that experience." Proffitt's reaction was that of a modest, generous man, who is eager to please his friends, and entertains no thought of personal reward. The discovery that he was able to give them something, equal in value to a fine guitar, was overwhelming.

Abrams and Warner were students of Brown at Duke, and they continued their interest in folk music after graduation. While he was in college, Warner, a talented musician, would accompany Brown on his folk music lectures, to illustrate the songs.

Shortly after Brown and Abrams first visited Proffitt in 1938, Warner came to Pick Britches Valley to collect folk songs from Nathan Hicks and his family. It was on this trip that Warner met Proffitt, Hicks's son-in-law, and learned of his banjo-making. He collected the Tom Dooley song on the first visit; on succeeding visits, he collected a total of 119 songs from Proffitt.

Proffitt is credited as the source of the version of Tom Dooley that appears in Lomax's collection *(Folk Songs, USA)*, and on a Frank Warner recording made for Elektra Records. That record is now out of print, but several of Proffitt's songs appear on Warner's "Our Singing Heritage, Vol. III," also an Elektra record.

Carl Sandburg recommends this recording "for those wanting to hear an authentic folk singer." I recommend it for family listening if you just want to have an evening of good fun.

VIII.

Proffitt feels a closeness to Tom Dula (which is pronounced Dooley in the mountains), partly because his grandmother knew him and partly because Tom was a banjo-player and ballad singer. As Proffitt puts it:

"Never admiring the deed that was said he done, I did from a boy up have a warm spot for the humble way he accepted his death, by playing his banjo and singing:
"I'll take down my banjo and
  pick it on my knee
'This time tommorrow, h'it'll
  be no use to me.' "

"In a few simple words," Proffitt said, "Tom made a ballad that will live with the others he loved to sing and redeemed himself as far as it was possible to do so."

Alan Lomax wrote that "one should perhaps never say he knows a folk song. At best one can know a variant or variants of it."

Proffitt bears this out; the version he quoted above is

but one of "two or three differences in the song I get."

Folk singers are very susceptible to suggestions. Since the Kingston Trio recording of "Tom Dooley" became so popular, Proffitt has to listen to the Frank Warner recording, on which Warner emulates Proffitt, in order "to get clear in my mind the old way I sang it."

The Tom Dooley legend was told to him by his grandmother, Adeline Pardue Proffitt, who came from down in Happy Valley, where Laura Foster lived. According to her version, Tom composed the song himself.

The actual killing had all of the best elements for making a folk ballad. Tom was a Confederate hero, and quite popular with the women. Laura was his beautiful sweetheart, and Anne Melton was the equally beautiful "other woman," who was held for trial but released. She is said to have told the court, "You'll never put a rope around this pretty neck."

There was, and still is, speculation that Anne did the actual killing, and some of the versions of the ballad express doubt about Tom's guilt. The alleged cause of the killing was brought out during Tom's two trials, at which he was defended by Zeb Vance, his former commanding officer. I prefer the romantic version of the motive, but if you prefer accuracy, consult Brown's Collection of *North Carolina Folklore,* Vol. II, pages 703-714.

Except for the motive, a story told me by a Ferguson native tallies pretty well with Brown's account, based on newspaper reports of that day.

IX.

After leaving Proffitt, I spent the night in Boone, and the next day visited with Dr. Williams, who directed me to some of the literature on folk music, much of which is in the Appalachian Library. The following day I visited the graves of Laura Foster and Tom Dula.

Laura's grave is located near Happy Valley, in a cultivated field right off Highway 268. Her home was not far away. Tom's grave is several miles off the highway, down at Ferguson.

Near Laura's grave, I stopped and talked with Robert Glenn McNeil, who told me that his father had been in the party that found Laura's grave. On the spot where her blood was spilled, McNeil said, there is a sourwood that was young when her father helped discover the body. It's never grown a bit, McNeil reported.

At a rural pool room at Ferguson, I made the chance acquaintance of Chelsie Groce, a timber cutter. Groce added a witness to the killing. Like most people in the area, he speaks of the murder, which took place in 1865, as if it were yesterday. Groce talked with such conviction that I decided to accept his account.

His Grandfather Welch, who died in his 90's when Groce was 8, was a first cousin to Laura and Tom. Pearline Scott, a schoolmate of another of Groce's long-lived ancestors, witnessed the killing. (Groce is such an accomplished, and rapid, story-teller that I lost the genealogy in muddled notes, and finally gave up note-taking altogether.)

Pearline confided in her schoolmate, who told the story to Groce many times.

Pearline, Tom, and Anne met Laura on a mountainside. If the meeting was by design, Pearline didn't know it. Anne and Tom engaged Laura in an argument while Pearline stayed out of hearing. Suddenly, Tom grabbed Laura's arms and pinned them behind her, and Anne "stobbed" her with a knife.

"Laura fell," Groce said, "and they run off a-ways. Then Tom come back and beat her in the head with a pine knot."

According to Groce, Laura had three burials. Tom buried her first in a swampy place. He had to break her legs to get her into the grave. He dug her up again and buried her on what is now known as Laura's Ridge.

"They say that a horse in the search party balked at her grave, and that's the way they found it," Groce said, "but that's not so. Pearline Scott took them to the grave."

The rest is record. Tom and Anne were indicted in Wilkes County in the fall of 1866; the trial was moved to Statesville, in Iredell County, where Governor Vance moved for a severance. Tom was tried separately, convicted, sentenced to die, won a new trial, and was convicted a second time.

He was hanged at Statesville 2:17 p.m. on May 1, 1868, after having signed a statement that he alone killed Laura.

Anne's pretty neck never stretched rope, but they say when she lay dying, you could hear the sizzling of meat, so close was she to her reward.

July and August 1960

TOUCH WOOD FOR LUCK

By Edward E. Brown, Jr.

How many times have you boasted about something and then "Knock on wood" to ward off punishment for boasting? If you have you're not alone for one of the most prevalent of all superstitions is for people to invariably knock on wood after bragging about their success or good health.

In February, 1940, when Winston Churchill was First Lord of the Admiralty, he told the House of Commons that up to that date only the battleship "Royal Oak" and the aircraft carrier "Courageous" of the British fleet had been sunk during the war. Ellen Wilkinson, a Labor member, shouted, "Touch Wood!"

"I sympathize with that feeling," replied Churchill. "I rarely like to be any considerable distance from a piece of wood" and touched his dispatch box.

How wood acquired this supposed protective power against misfortune and bad luck is not definitely known. One theory is that it came from the old game known as "Touching wood" or "wood tag," in which a player who succeeds in touching wood is safe from capture.

Another theory has it that this game and "knocking on wood" had a common origin in primitive tree worship, when trees were believed to harbor protective spirits. To rap on a tree was to call up the spirit of the tree to protect one against impending misfortune.

Later, people would place the hand on a wooden statue of a deity for the same purpose of warding off misfortune.

Some people hold the superstition to be of Christian origin and that it's in some way associated with the wooden cross upon which Jesus was crucified. Perhaps, they think, it's a survival of the religious rite of touching a crucifix when taking an oath or the beads of the rosary when praying.

Regardless of its origin, the superstition of knocking on wood is likely here to stay.

June 1970

SPRING IS A SLOW MULE

White is the color of dogwood, and pink, when the root is split, and purple's the wealth of richness by which spring is welcomed in thrift.

Sing out, and make your verses as you go. Now is the season for singing.

The man with the mule sang. He was plowing a garden in the backyard of a house on the east side of town. It wasn't much of a garden, but then the man with the mule didn't have much a song.

He was coming down the streets with his mule hitched to a lopsided wagon when he was hailed. He was riding on a board up front, slumped forward with the reins loosely held. Behind him were a plow and harrow. Both were brown with rust, and both were patched with rusted bailing wire.

He sang low, to himself. The song might have been a hymn. You couldn't tell. Perhaps he couldn't tell himself, and now and then he would break it off to holler to his mule.

The people for whom he was plowing hadn't asked his name, or where he lived, or where he was going when they saw him passing. He was the same man, though, they thought, who had come past last year and the year before. They never had known how to find him or telephone him; they waited until he happened by, and he always came about the same time of the year.

"How much?" they had asked him. "We just need a couple of rows. Not planning on anything but a few tomatoes. That's about all we can keep hoed."

106

Oh, about two dollars, he had answered. They weren't sure they wanted to pay more than a dollar and a half.

"Well, go ahead," they said. Since we stopped you, you might as well run off a couple of rows."

The man with the mule pulled into their drive and when the mule had been unhitched from the wagon and hitched to the plow, he went to work.

A neighbor of the people came over to watch. The neighbor wanted a garden plowed, too, and soon the man with the mule had agreed to take on that job and another farther down the street.

He plowed and he sang, low and softly to himself. Most people now had their gardens plowed by tractor, and many who once had gardens now had given them up. On the street where he worked now, a man for whom he once had plowed several years back was plowing for himself, walking behind a small garden tractor.

But he sang. Or perhaps it wasn't a song but a moan. In another year or so he wouldn't come that way. He was getting old, his mule was old. The plow and harrow wouldn't last much longer, nor would the wagon. And people weren't keeping gardens as they used to, not on that street.

When he was done with that yard and the others, it was nearly dark. He loaded the plow and harrow into the wagon, hitched the mule between the shafts and drove away, the wagon cracking and its rims crunching on the gravel, leaving behind a song of their own.

The people for whom he had plowed listened to him go. He'd be back, they told each other. He was like the birds that come back and the flowers. He'd come like the jonquils and the red japonica. You'd look out to the street one spring evening and there he'd be, passing with his mule and wagon. And then in no more time than it takes to plow a couple of rows he'd be gone again. Like the jonquils. With a low song.

Sing out, and make your verses as you go.

How soon the hasty daffodil, call it jonquil if you will, has given up its blossom. How soon then will the tulip come. How soon the beauty passes.

April 1967

"PROCLAMATION DAY"

Largely because various organizations, businesses and lobbying groups have managed over the years to build it into his job, a governor spends a lot of time proclaiming special observances, days, weeks, months and such. So many "proclamations" are issued and so many observances observed that they have lost all meaning and North Carolina's governor has to hold two Proclamation Days a month to take care of the signing and the attendant ceremony. Carolina Country sat in on a Proclamation Day session with the Governor. Here is how it went.

Governor Bob Scott sat behind his desk and, speaking as though he had an audience in his office, congratulated the people of South Carolina on their state's 300th anniversary.

"We in North Carolina are proud to have shared so much history with you," he said. "As two of the original 13 states we have much in common."

A television camera recorded the message for showing later over South Carolina television stations in connection with South Carolina's Tricentennial.

"A good take," the cameraman announced as he shut off his equipment. Congratulating Scott on a good performance, he began disconnecting his lights and cables.

It was 2 o'clock and the beginning of one of the two afternoon sessions the Governor and his press secretary, C.T. West, set aside each month for observing observances, designating special days, weeks and months and issuing special proclamations.

As the TV man packed up his gear, West brought in the first of six groups which had been waiting in the outer office and outside in the corridors and under the dome of the stately old Capitol.

The first group was made up of representatives of Toastmasters Clubs around the state and was accompanied by a photographer.

As the 10 or so members of the group arranged themselves for a picture, the Governor read the statement his office was issuing declaring May 1970 Toastmasters' Month in North Carolina.

Several photographs were made. The visitors shook hands with the Governor and the group left, carrying the official statement the Governor had signed. West followed the Toastmasters out to let the next group know the Governor was ready.

Waiting for it to arrive, the Governor said hundreds of organizations, businesses and associations and some individuals ask him to issue proclamations. Every governor had done it, he noted, and it takes up a lot of every governor's time.

In most cases, Scott said, we don't really issue proclamations; we issue statements. Proclamations, he explained, usually are issued only to declare official State holidays, bank holidays and such.

Last year, Governor Scott signed 143 statements and proclamations. At a "proclamation session" in March, he designated:

April 19-25 Youth Temperance Education Week.

April 4-11 Chamber of Commerce Week.

April 24-May 1 Medical Technologists Week.

April 22 Queen Isabella Day.

March 30-April 5 Future Business Leaders of America Week.

April 5-11 Life Insurance Week.

April 19-25 Dietetics Week.

At an earlier session, he designated 11 special observances for March.

There is a considerable amount of time to it, the Governor said, and I've debated whether it's worth the time. When you consider what the people of North Carolina pay their governors, it gets to be pretty expensive.

About three-fourths of a governor's time is taken up like this, he added. It's work anybody can do, but people seem to want the governor to do it.

The next group, a sizeable delegation representing the North Carolina Poultry Federation, began filing in. Like every other group that afternoon, the Poultry people brought along a photographer. They were also accompanied by a farm editor and a television man.

After everybody had been introduced, two attractive young women in the delegation presented the governor with several one dozen cartons of eggs and a platter piled high with turkey sausages in fresh rolls. Pictures were made of the Governor sampling the turkey sausage. He pronounced it very tasty.

Settling again in his big chair, the Governor signed an impressive document designating April 1970 as Poultry Products Month in North Carolina and extolling the importance of the poultry industry to North Carolina's agribusiness economy.

As the cameras clicked and the television man did his silent bit, the Governor was presented a five pound carton of chicken drumsticks, a 13.5 pound dressed young turkey, a five pound carton of frying chicken parts and a six pound breast of chicken roll.

Scott told his visitors he was particularly appreciative because the poultry products could all be used at the Mansion.

It will help the budget, he joked, and will come in

handy for all the luncheons and teas that are held there, as well as for regular Mansion meals.

A delegation representing North Carolina's textile manufacturing industry came in next. It brought not only its own photographer but its own writer, plus about eight five-yard lengths of the latest dress and shirt materials and enough fine fabric to make a man's suit.

In conversations with the Governor, members of the group made the point repeatedly that Japanese textiles are flooding the American market, driving North Carolina textile workers out of jobs and North Carolina mills out of business. The Governor listened sympathetically and made agreeable small talk. (On other occasions, under similar circumstances, farm commodity groups and businesses seeking to expand foreign trade and improve foreign markets for their products have and would lobby gently for less restriction in world trade.)

Then, getting down to the real business at hand, the textile executives posed with the Governor as he signed a statement designating April 1970 as Textile Futures Month in North Carolina. The document endorsed an "Operation Futures" program to encourage young people to pursue textile careers.

In the wake of the textile group's departure, two of the Governor's top aides, David Murray and Ben Roney, entered, each with an urgent item of official business. Quickly facts were reported, developments considered and decisions made.

Three girls and four boys representing the Youth Councils of North Carolina came in. The seven high school seniors from various sections of the state had come with a photographer and a local TV newsman to have the Governor designate April 27-May 3 as Youth Week. Scott signed an appropriately worded official document for them, told them he was making plans for a State Youth Conference to be held in the fall, and gave each a card bearing the State seal on which he quickly wrote each a personal message as a souvenir.

The students told the Governor North Carolina is the only state to have a statewide youth organization such as theirs. That started a conversation in which Scott referred to many other things in which North Carolina is either "only" or "first."

North Carolina, Scott reminded the students, has achieved many firsts in education. He gave some examples, and the students gave others.

And so it went. After the students, a Mrs. David Glass of Kannapolis came in for the North Carolina Federation of Women's Clubs with a photographer. The photographer took her picture with Scott as the Governor signed a statement designating May 1 as Youth Conservation Day. Mrs. Glass and Scott exchanged pleasantries as she left, telling him she would see him at the Federation's state convention.

Finally, four smartly dressed ladies, all in gay spring outfits and hats, entered carrying small flower-trimmed baskets on their arms. As their photographer snapped pictures, the Governor signed a document for them designating May 17-23 Welcome Wagon Week. They told Scott the baskets were their "trademark" and said Welcome Wagon ladies welcome thousands of new people, many from out of state, to new homes in North Carolina communities.

They badly wanted the Governor to come to their convention. The Governor had an out of state engagement on their meeting date, but he said he hoped they'd ask him again next year.

It was now approaching 3:40 p.m. The day's session had run a bit shorter than the usual two hours.

One of these days, the Governor said, we're going to
have C. T. (West) issue a proclamation for Proclamation
Day.

June 1970

A FEW PETUNIAS TO REMEMBER

Every house in the block is gone. All that remains to show there once were houses are the now filled-in depressions of their foundations, an occasional set of concrete steps and a few petunias.

They grow, these straggling petunias, by a set of the old concrete steps, plaintive yet gay, reminding passers-by that here in another spring people lived, trees and grass grew and children played; reminding those whose minds turn to such things that a part of the city had been swept away.

The block was dying long before the wreckers came. Its houses were decaying. Porches sagged. Paint peeled. Windows and weatherboarding showed chronic neglect. The people who built the houses were long gone. The homes in which they had taken pride saw their last days as rental property and boarding houses, and decaying people lived among the decay, with cans and bottles in what had been lawns, and looked out over litter in the street.

A strong new public building will rise soon on the block, and grass and trees will grow again. The fine days when the houses were new, and the last days when they were old and dying, all will be forgotten.

And perhaps the petunias will be forgotten, too. Perhaps some builders' workman, digging for new foundations, will trample them and they will be buried in the clay.

But, and it could be, perhaps some wiser hand will make a place in future plans, among the shrubs and more pretentious plantings, for one small bed so that when the great new building is complete, a few petunias will grow there remembering at its feet.

July 1967

THE GLORIOUS FOURTH

The most glorious of American holidays creeps across the calendar these days almost as surreptiously as Shrove Tuesday.

Oldtimers, who recall the days when a Fourth of July was a whizzbang of a celebration, complain the present generation doesn't give the day its due.

"It wasn't always so," they lament. And Raleigh history bears them out.

In Raleigh's infancy, the Fourth began with a cannonade and ended with a dance.

The *Raleigh Register and North Carolina Weekly Advertiser* of Tuesday, July 8, 1800, which gave four of its 20 columns to reprinting the Declaration of Independence, recorded Raleigh turned out in its best for Fourth of July that year.

"Friday past being the anniversary of American independence — a day dear to all true patriots as it rescued their country from the fangs of arbitrary power — was observed here with due respect," the paper reported. Due respect in those times meant a day of toasts and cannon salutes.

"The festival was announced at the break of day by the firing of cannon, and at 2 o'clock about 60 of the citizens assembled at Captain Rogers' spring in the vicinity of the city where a temporary canopy was erected and an elegant cold collation was provided by Mr. Casso, the arrangements of which reflected high credit upon him."

Mr. Casso, supplier of the elegant collation, was operator of the same tavern in whose courtyard young Andrew Johnson, a future president, was born.

"The company being seated," the account continued, "Governor Williams as president (of the occasion) and Colonel Polk (who later was to become the nation's 11th president) as vice president, the Declaration of Independence was read. After dining, the following toasts were given, each of which was announced by a different charge of cannon.

"Between the toasts a number of patriotic and convivial songs were sung and the day passed away in undisturbed harmony — no party spirit, that demon of discord, pervaded the meeting.

"The shades of evening alone warned the company to separate; when the president, vice president and gentlemen present repaired to the State House to meet the ladies of the city, where an elegant collation was provided and the 'mazy dance succeeded the flowing bowl.' "

A total of 16 toasts was drunk that Fourth of July, though the paper fails to say in what beverage, and after each the cannoneers would fire at will. Upon to 16 salutes were fired if the gunners felt the toast warranted. Guns and toasters must have been warm by the end of the day.

The toasts raised July 4, 1800 were as all-inclusive as a political platform.

The *Raleigh Register* listed them all:

"1. The Day — the auspicious Fourth of July — may it ever be held in remembrance by the sons of America as the day of their political freedom.

"2. The memory of George Washington.

"3. The heroes who fell in the Revolutionary War — may their memory be an incentive to their successors.

"4. The United States — may they continue free, sovereign and independent; not influenced by foreign intrigue nor disturbed by internal confusion.

"5. The President of the United States — may his

117

countrymen rightly appreciate his distinguished virtue, patriotism and firmness.

"6. The Vice President of the United States.

"7. Both Houses of Congress and judicial officers of the United States.

"8. The Militia of the United States — may the valour of the soldier be combined with the virtue of the citizen.

"9. The Navy of the United States — the benefits which have risen from its infant efforts are a just presage of its future greatness and usefulness.

"10. Agriculture and Commerce — may they both have the fostering hand of government (imagine today's self-styled defenders of free enterprise drinking to that), and as they are equally dependent on each other, so let them be equally regarded.

"11. Our Envoys Davie, Ellsworth, Murray — may their missions be crowned with success.

"12. The freedom of the press without licientuousness.

"13. The friends of religion and order — may they always triumph over the supporters of infidelity and confusion.

"14. The State of North Carolina.

"15. The University of North Carolina.

"16. The Americans fair — may their smiles excite deeds of valour in the youth of their country."

That might have been enough for any celebration — but it wasn't. The company, according to the *Raleigh Register*, was just getting warm.

"After the above," the paper adds, "several excellent volunteer toasts were drank."

The next year, and for years after, barring the period of the Civil War and the toastless days of the Reconstruction, the custom was repeated with varied vigor. Although the toasts have passed from memory and the cannons gave way

118

to firecrackers, North Carolina sustained its Fourth of July spirit until comparatively recent years.

Some think the arrival of the automobile and the popularity of trips to the beach and mountains are responsible for the current lack of ceremony.

But there are those who think a little of the old Fourth of July oratory these days might be just what the country needs. They want more of the old fire and vinegar and more of the old time toasts such as these:

"To the Habeas Corpus, the trial by jury, the freedom of the press and religion — may they be ever held sacred."

Or, "The Great Family of Man, may it live in Peace forever."

And once in a while, it might be a good idea to raise that old favorite:

"To the admirers of Monarchy; may they soon be enabled to leave us and go where they anticipate its blessings and protection," followed by 16 charges on the city's cannons.

The words could be changed a little, maybe, but no nation as young as ours is too old for a little celebration of its birth.

"HAPPY BIRTHDAY, REA"

By Bryan Haislip

A friend of mine had a birthday in May and I want to celebrate.

It means a lot to me because this particular friend helped me out when I was a boy. Maybe it wouldn't be too much to say that it changed the way of life down on the farm near Oak City for me and my family.

The friend I'm talking about is the North Carolina Rural Electrification Authority. An act of the General Assembly, ratified May 3, 1935, created the REA as a State agency.

In those days only 3.2 percent of North Carolina farms had electricity. We were in the other 96.8 percent down in eastern Martin County. It was a little better for the U.S. as a whole, with 10.9 percent of the farms on power lines, but it was just assumed that one of the differences between living in town and living in the country was electric lights.

Today 99 percent of Tar Heel farms have electric service, ahead of the national average of 98.4. Electric membership corporations organized under the North Carolina REA program are serving more than 260,000 families and 10,000 businesses and industries.

David Hamil, the U.S. Rural Electrification Administrator, recently reported more than 320,000 North Carolina electric consumers and 96,000 telephone subscribers are served by REA borrowers.

My children read the statistics, but they don't really see the picture. An ice storm knocked out the power a couple of years ago.

They thought it was great fun — warming by the

fireplace, cooking over the coals, using candles for light. "Just like the old days," my daughter said smugly. The novelty wore thin the second day and power finally was restored before everbody's nerves snapped.

When I was a teenager — I didn't know I was because the word wasn't invented; I thought I was still a child which shows the innocence of the time — when I was my children's age, it was my job to get up first, light the lamp, build the fire in the stove and bring water from the well. Not bad chores in summer but something else again in a house cold from a winter night, and frost rim white on the well chain.

The Edgecombe-Martin County Electric Membership Corporation was organized and chartered in 1936. Its first project, on a loan of $32,000 was 32 miles of line to serve 87 farm consumers completed in April, 1937.

It was a great day, and even better at night. The house blazed with light. Bare bulbs hung on drop cords from the middle of the ceiling and today you'd think it made an awful glare. We didn't.

"Gee," said my sister. "It's like having an Alladin lamp in every room."

I won't even try to explain what an Alladin lamp was, only to say it gave a whiter light than a kerosene lamp, but still nothing like a 60-watt bulb.

That was the beginning. A refrigerator, a stove (Mother kept the wood stove on the other side of the kitchen and made the transition by degrees), an electric iron — all the things electricity made possible for convenience and better living followed in turn. Indoor plumbing ended my early morning trips to the well. My friend REA had taken over my onerous chores.

Gwyn B. Price, an Ashe County farmer and teacher, was named chairman of the North Carolina Rural Electrification

Authority by the late Gov. J. Melville Broughton in 1941, six years after the creation of the agency. He's continued to hold the job under seven succeeding governors, directing the widening service of REA.

The Biblical three score and 10 divided by half is 35 which ought to mean that middle-age begins on that birthday. Not for REA; it remains vigorous and ready for challenges.

Governor Scott tossed a new — rural housing — to it this spring in a speech to the Tarheel Electric Membership Association.

"I am calling upon you, the rural electric cooperatives, to assume the leadership in identifying the housing problems in your areas, in calling together other interested citizens to identify and work on problems inhibiting housing development and in working with state and federal agencies to take advantage of every program available," he said.

That's a story for the future. My greeting is for the accomplishments of the past, a 35-year record of achievement in bringing light and power to rural North Carolina.

Happy Birthday, REA!

July 1970

WHEN IT'S AUGUST

A hot breath blows across the
land
And cows stand cooling in the
creek
And weekend crowds bake upon
the beach
Or take to camps and mountain
rendezvous.
Now lakes echo sounds of
motorboats
And flash with spray from
skimming water skis.
At tables under churchyard trees
Congregations eat homecoming
feasts.
And farmers take the measure
of their crops,
Searching skies against the
chance of hail.
Here and there, dogs curl in the
shade
And small boys count the days
till school.
For now is summer at its height
When August is the calendar's
name;
For summer's most and soon the
summer's end.

BIRD CALLS AT DAWN

Hear how the birds call.
As darkness fades with daybreak,
As the day begins,
They greet the spreading dawn,
Calling in their trills as sleeping trees
Are washed in the morning's light;
Calling as though they, these birds,
Were heralds of the sun;
Singing as though they were to wake the flowers.
Trilling, chirping, calling, singing;
A medley in many notes and keys,
As though they knew this is the day,
Like every day when hopes rise
Fresh with each new dawn;
That this is a day
Like every day each of us is given
To turn away from yesterday's regrets;
To amend its errors and build anew
From its mistakes
To make a better tomorrow.

THE BIGGEST FISH ARE STILL UNCAUGHT

It's a rarer sight than it was when we were younger to see young boys quietly fishing. Nowadays boys — and girls too — often favor livelier pleasures. But the fish are still there, and the biggest are still to be caught, and boys are still boys for all the changes in the world around us. And it is we who err and not they if we judge them and their generation without remembering that another generation might ask if ours has done as well as we expect of theirs. of theirs.

Remember how it was when you were young. . . when you were 12 or 14 and wondering if you'd ever grow up? Remember how you and a friend would go down to the creek, or to the river if there was a river near, and how you would sit on the bank and fish and talk?

Remember?

It was a special thing to do. You couldn't just go whenever you took a notion. The wood box had to be full behind the big iron range in the kitchen. Kindling had to be cut to start the fire next day for breakfast. The kerosene lamps had to be filled, and fresh water put out for the chickens. You had to have your work caught up so your mother and father would let you go.

You'd take your poles and your cans of worms and you'd walk barefooted taking the shortest way and yet picking the softest places to step, avoiding the sandburs and the stubble. And your dog and your friend's dog would come with you, following behind or running ahead, stopping now and then to explore and sniffing and panting as dogs do.

When you'd come to the place where you thought your fishing luck was best, you'd bait your hooks and you would dangle your lines at the ends of your poles into the water. And you would hold your poles so that your corks would float freely on the surface, And you would find a place to sit and watch for your corks to bob and to wait for the sudden pulls on the end of the lines which meant fish had taken your hooks.

Remember?

Remember how clear the water was — before so many streams were polluted. You could see the bottom in many places. You could see the fish swimming, or darting suddenly, or resting lazily in the shadows. And water bugs would scurry on the surface and dragonflies would flit about and you would hear birds calling and a crow far off.

And when you caught a fish, you would flip it up on the bank and it would squirm and flap in the leaves until you could take it from the hook, and you'd bet your friend the next one you caught would be bigger.

Those were days to cherish. They were days when the first World War had been won and Hitler hadn't got around yet to starting World War II, and when there still were many people who had most of the other things people were supposed to have to live right but who hadn't yet got electricity or a car and didn't soon expect to.

They were days when boys like you, sitting on the bank, fishing and talking quietly, so quietly that if fish had ears they could not hear, would share the many bits of knowledge boys had ways of knowing then. Like how a boy you knew at school was going to get a bike by selling salve, and what bikes were best, and how far you could shoot with a BB gun, or who had just got a new team of mules. And like what was the strongest, a tiger or a lion, and who was the greatest ace in the dogfights over France, and what was the fastest, a motorcycle or a car.

Sometimes when we recall it all, we may wonder if boys today still know such pleasures and whether our sons and daughters are growing up too fast and are living too easily and are missing the things we valued so.

When we find our thoughts running that way we can know we are growing old too fast and that we are forgetting how it is to be a boy fishing on the bank.

Because there are many ways for boys — and girls too — to fish without fishing, to talk and to let their thoughts wander and to explore the things important to them without sitting on a bank with a pole. And our sons, even as we did before them, have ways of knowing special things. Like whether the Kools or the Animals, or is it the Beatles, made the top hit song, and what electric guitar is the most, and which engine is the fastest, and which sports car is the best on curves, and what astronaut was the first to walk in space.

They don't have to split kindling or build the fire for breakfast, and they take electricity, like television and jet planes, for granted. They may not know the things we knew but they know other things which we as boys never could have imagined.

And who's to say that the things we knew when we were 12 were more meaningful than the things they know?

And who's to judge whether the kind of world our generation has created for them to grow up in is a better world because we fished on the bank or will be better or worse than they will bring about for the children they someday will father?

"LEAVE THE MAYONNAISE OFF"

By Dick Pence

You'd think that after nearly three years in this state, I'd eventually learn how to order an egg sandwich — and get what I want.

On the contrary, ordering egg sandwiches has become such an ordeal that I've considered even the drastic possibility of omitting them from my list of desirable snacks.

Not that it's the fault of the egg sandwich. Far be it — it's a delightful morsel. Nor can it be blamed on the waitress who takes my order or the cook who prepares it.

And I don't think it's really my fault.

Right now, stop a second and picture an egg sandwich. Got it? Looks good, doesn't it? But what I really want to know is how you made that sandwich. Is it toasted or untoasted? Buttered or with mayonnaise?

Before you go off to the kitchen to get something to eat, let me illustrate my problem.

One evening some time back, I dropped into a nearby restaurant where I often eat.

After looking over the same menu I'd seen at least a couple of hundred times, my appetite diminished and I decided to have just a sandwich and a glass of milk.

"Give me an egg sandwich and a glass of milk," I said to the waitress.

"One egg sandwich and a glass of milk," she repeated, first to me and then to the cook.

Here's what arrived at my table a little later: a fried egg, liberally smeared with mayonnaise, and placed between two slices of toasted bread.

129

That, of course, is an egg sandwich. It may be exactly what you thought of a few sentences back. And I'm sure the cook felt he had filled my order to the letter.

Unfortunately, he hadn't. According to me, this is an egg sandwich: a fried egg placed between two buttered slices of untoasted white bread.

Before I go any further, let me say that I definitely do not want to be drawn into an ideological discussion on the relative merits of toast and mayonnaise over plain bread and butter, or vice versa. The point I want to make is simply the words "egg sandwich" mean something different to me than they do to the cook, or even you.

Why? About all I can say is that, for some reason, in the Midwest sandwiches are made with untoasted bread and butter, and in the South they are invariably constructed with toasted bread and mayonnaise.

About now you probably want to point out the obvious solution to the egg sandwich problem. Tell the waitress exactly how you like it prepared.

Well, after a while even I was clever enough to figure out this solution.

So the next time I wanted an egg sandwich, I cleared my throat, took a deep breath, and said: "Please give me one fried egg sandwich on white bread with butter, don't toast it and leave the mayonnaise off."

Then I sat back smugly until my order arrived. This is what I got: one fried egg placed neatly on some slice of bread (toasted on one side), two patties or margarine and one small paper container filled with mayonnaise.

This incident has convinced me that the idea of buttered, untoasted egg sandwiches is too horrendous for some Southerners to even comprehend. (This is somewhat akin to my feelings about mayonnaise on eggs.)

At one time I thought I might conceivably have the egg

sandwich problem solved. After several ennervating rounds, I managed to teach the cook in one local restaurant how to make a Midwestern-style egg sandwich.

And he does a very good job of it. However, I find it quite discomforting to eat such sandwiches while the waitresses whisper and giggle and look sideways at me.

It all comes down to the fact that fried egg sandwiches have become the very symbol of my non-North Carolina background — to the point that I have decided I will no longer betray myself by recognizing their existence in public.

I'm not going to let that keep me from eating egg sandwiches, though. In the future when I crave one, I will make it under cover of darkness in my own kitchen.

In another year or two I expect to master the art of flipping a frying egg without having it disintegrate before my eyes.

September 1961

LET THE BUYER BEWARE

Once when socks were sized to fit the foot, a man could wear hosiery and still wiggle his toes.

He can't anymore. A masterpiece of mass produced ingenuity called the stretch sock has squeezed the familiar sizes into small, medium and large, and the average American male now toes the line for progress.

Progress is what such inventiveness is supposed to represent. Progress it may be. But there may be more than mere coincidence in the fact that it is an inventiveness which seems to serve commerce more than it benefits consumers.

In the case of socks, innovation has simplified manufacturing and merchandising problems by eliminating sizes. All goes well until the socks are washed. The stretch then becomes the bind and toes are tortured more each time the socks come from the clothesline. . . oops, pardon, the dryer.

So it is also with nearly everything from automobiles to electronic products to margarine.

The big thing now in automobiles is unitized construction. It reduces manufacturing costs by substituting automatic welding for the more expensive nut and bolt assembly. It results, if so much as a fender is dented, in much more expensive repairs.

In the electronic orbit, the new way is printed circuits. They cut production costs, but they produce complexities when the works must be repaired.

What has happened with margarine shows how the giant economy package can be less economical than the smaller family size, or how 16 ounces can be made to add up to something more than a pound. Until recently a pound package of margarine contained four four-ounce sticks. Now some of them are containing six. There still are only 16 ounces in the package but, by a bit of applied sales psychology, the shopper is made to think she's getting a bonus.

There used to be an expression that what is new is "a change for the better." Progress makes an even older expression apply.

"Caveat emptor," the wily Romans warned. In 1968, the Latin translates with ageless aptness, "Let the buyer beware."

WHEN NATURE SPEAKS

What is it that birds say
In the early dawn
Before the sun is up?
You hear them chattering;
Chattering and warbling in brief calls.
Is it different really
Than what birds say at dusk?
Is the dawn talk
Nature's greeting to the sun?
And the dusk talk
Nature's evening prayer?
Who would know unless he listens?
Who would know unless he cares?

THE ANIMAL KINGDOM

By Lodwick Hartley

I built a house in a small forest not because I had a Thoreau-like yearning to live close to nature but rather because lots on the pavement were at least three times more expensive. However, there were specious natural attractions about the location I chose. It was heavily wooded, and it was bounded on one side by a clear and energetic little stream flowing from a spring on a nearby hillside. Birds of many varieties sang in the overhanging branches, and squirrels chatted as they spiraled around the tree trunks. One day (in the mating season, I presume) I even saw two small turtles lumbering across the pine needles in a slow-motion parody of the romantic pursuit. In short, the place seemed to have much to offer in the way of the bucolic and idyllic.

My initial assumption about a house — one, I have discovered, not entirely shared by contemporary architects — was that it made a distinct definition of indoors as opposed to outdoors, that it shut the inside in and the outside out, except on those occasions when by sufferance of the tenant the outside was allowed a controlled function in promoting his convenience in matters of ventilation and lighting, and in providing a bit of natural scenery now and then to supplement the etchings and the wallpaper. I had only to become a occupant of my "shelter" to discover that nature. regardless of what architectural faith one may profess, is perversely not subject to control or definition, that trees with all their outward show of benevolence can be first-class pains in the neck, that the gentle rain falling

135

from heaven can have something less than a quality of mercy, and that the dear little creatures of the woods so cunningly depicted by illustrators of childrens' books are often sinister enemies of man's peace and comfort.

I shall not concern myself here with such a universal minor nuisance as that of woodpeckers stupidly beating an early morning tattoo on the tin gutters. Nor shall I linger over the equally common and by no means unexpected invasion of my privacy early in the game by a mouse that, before it was handily caught, did no more serious damage than decorating two candles with a delightfully intricate pattern of teeth marks and consuming, with inexplicable gout, the fringe of a none too decorative pillow.

The first really shocking suggestion that I might not be allowed to live alone and like it came one summer afternoon after I had bidden goodbye to two friends who had dropped in for a brief visit and who had had with me one sedate round of a long cool drink on my terrace the size of a cocktail napkin. On a routine check of my plumbing facilities, I was not a little astounded to find a scattering of black spots on the pristing white cover of what the British, without false modesty, call the w.c. Instinctively, I examined the open window to see whether soot could have blown in; but I quickly realized that there could be no soot in mid-summer in an all but primeval forest. I next looked upward to the ceiling for any possible crack in the plaster. There was none.

When I looked down again, I was further astonished to see on the porcelain neck between the cover and the tank what looked like a sizeable piece of electric cable. The whole situation made absolutely no sense at all, and I began to wonder whether the long cool drink had been as mild as I had had every intention of making it.

Without further argument with myself, I reached down

to remove the cable. I had no sooner grasped it than I discovered that I had picked up a snake about two and a half feet long.

Now it turned out to be merely a little black snake (Zamenis constrictor, as it is described in the books), perfectly harmless and capable, I am told, of being a valuable friend in consuming rodents and in keeping one's premises free of venomous crawling things. ("Most snakes are not only harmless to man," says the unabridged Webster, "but often useful.") But at the time I had no inclination to identify my visitor or to accept a friendship so informally proffered. All that I could think in a moment of terror was that a snake is a snake; and I consequently dropped the creature as if it had been molten lead, jumping as I did so to the edge of the tub, where I stood swinging to the rod of the shower curtain until I could survey the situation with more equanimity.

I regret to say that the only way I could figure out to rid myself of this "friend to man" was to get a hoe and kill it. I promptly did so. And even when I found and sealed the loose plywood covering left by the plumbers in the linen closet for convenient access to the newly installed pipes and thus solved the mystery of the snake's point of entry (and, incidentally, of the tar spots on the w.c. cover), I was in no state of mind for enjoying the comforts of home in complete relaxation. For months I never opened the bathroom door without expecting to be greeted with a hiss or a rattle; and I nightly probed the fuzzy dust under my bed with pious zeal.

With the coming of winter my queasiness began to subside in the knowledge that hibernation is an established social custom among both the least and the most respectable of the ophidians; and sound sleep, unplagued by snake dreams of entirely un-Freudian significance, was again the rule under a roof that had not yet begun to leak.

I was not again frightened out of my wits until a cold night in January. About twelve thirty o'clock in the very midst of that sweet first sleep that comes after the book has fallen shut of its own weight and the bedside lamp has been extinguished by a gently groping hand, I was awakened by what sounded like footsteps in my living room. My internal thermostat promptly shot downward and I froze.

"At last, a burglar." I though, realizing for the first time that my boast to my friends about having no fear of living in comparative isolation had been an ill-founded one.

Perhaps I found some comfort in recognizing that my lack of any protective implement other than a dull kitchen knife in a drawer that I could not possibly reach was a blessing rather than a bane, and in remembering that the best course of action in any event was to pretend that I was sound asleep. So I lay perfectly still.

Clump-clump-clump continued the noise from the living room. For fully ten minutes the sound came at irregular and, what I eventually decided to be, singularly peculiar intervals for a two-footed marauder of efficient working habits. As my reasoning powers returned, I began to thaw. No halfway sensible burglar, I argued, would spend valuable time making a leisurely promenade of my living room where the only things of value were a few books that (unless, indeed, he were an exceptional burglar like John Shand in a famous play of Barrie) could have no meaning to him.

So I gathered the courage to get up and make an inspection of the room from which the disturbance was coming. I did so in full light and found nothing to indicate the presence of a living creature. Furthermore, there was the complete silence of a very cold night both inside and outside.

Of course, the only thing needed to bring about a continuation of the noise was my return to bed; and the only thing necessary to produce dead silence again was another hurried inspection of the living room. By the time I had rushed from my bed to the living room a half dozen times I was properly incensed and just as properly determined to find the source of the annoyance. A long vigil established in pitch-black and reasonably cold dark eventually established the fact that the noise was coming from the mechanical draft in the grate, now securely closed because it had not recently been in use.

A squirrel, I surmised. It had ventured down the chimney and because of the closed draft it was thrashing about in an appropriate cul-de-sac. Well, it could find its own way out!

I assumed that if I opened from the mechanical draft and at the same time left the door to the terrace ajar, propping the screen door open to assure adequate egress, the native intelligence of any animal would enable it to make a comfortable escape.

For over an hour the avenue of escape was as wide open and as plainly marked as I could make it. Convinced that the squirrel had returned to its own nest, I finally got up and closed the door. After all, I did not want to have icicles all over the house the next morning. But no sooner had I settled down to sleep again than a series of metallic sounds assured me that the animal was going to have his fun in the chimney for the rest of the night. "O.K., let him!" I muttered, pulling the covers over my head in a grim effort to get a little sleep before dawn.

When I left groggily for work the next morning, everything was peaceful in the chimney. Having kept me awake for most of the night, the squirrel was luxuriating in contented slumber. Though I did not place on the hearth a dainty breakfast tray of acorns and assorted nuts for my guest, I did leave the draft open, thus giving him free access to my quarters.

Upon my return home from the office in the late afternoon, I immediately looked for a sign of my visitor. There was none. By this time I was more than ever determined to get some action; so I bent a coat hanger and began a probing operation in the chimney above the louvers of the draft — with absolutely no results.

Now I began to fear for the life of the squirrel, not because I had the least love or affection for the beast but because I did not relish the idea of having a decomposing corpse lodged in my chimney in such a way that only a team of brick masons could remove it. In frustration and indignation I dressed and went out for an evening appointment.

At ten-thirty or thereabouts I returned home. As I walked through the kitchen on my way from the garage to my bedroom, I discovered a pool of water on the floor. An oversize vase on the breakfast table had been upset and a general mess had been made with the flowers and the water. My guest had finally grown thirsty and had come out for a drink. He had accomplished his purpose the hard way — especially for me; and he had achieved a reasonable facsimile of the spillway at Grand Coulee in the process.

Before I could do anything else, I had to rush around with mops and towels in an effort to prevent permanent damage to the table and to the floor.

My swabbing of the deck having been accomplished, I was free to search for my little friend. Obviously, he was not now in the kitchen. Neither was he in the living room, as a thorough search seemed to indicate. But in my bedroom I had no sooner turned on the light than I saw a pair of eyes glistening brightly from a small brown mass in the corner.

140

A baby squirrel, I guessed at first. Poor little fellow, this will be easy, I thought.

"Now, my young man," I said audibly. "If you will not think me inhospitable, I'd like you to terminate your visit and run right back to your mamma and papa. They're probably wondering where the hell you are anyway."

The little squirrel cocked his head to one side with an air of pert incomprehension of my brashly patronizing speech. Then the pertness gave way to action. With a twitch of his body and tail, he was up the curtain of a nearby window in less than a flash. From the top of the cornice he sized up the situation quickly and then came at me in a totally unexpected dive-bombing attack.

He was not a baby squirrel after all, but a full-grown flying squirrel (Sciuropterus volucella) equipped with a jet motor aft!

I got out of the way as quickly as I could. In a moment, he had sped across the room, had flashed up another curtain, and had launched another attack at me.

Thoroughly taken aback by the ferocity of the little animal, I sought wildly for some kind of defensive weapon. In a hall closet I found a broom — a field piece, I later discovered, that can be disastrously clumsy when manipulated in a limited area.

Armed with the broom, I chased the squirrel back into the living room, and a duel of epic proportions began. It was not Achilles and Hector or Aeneas and Turnus, though the length and ferocity of the battle bore some similarity to that of the latter two. Perhaps it was more like David and Goliath — a jet-propelled David and a Goliath with a broom.

Under a sofa my antagonist would skitter, pausing long enough to get me within range, then whizzing at me at ankle length. Or up the curtain he would go for a

141

dive-bombing attack. Up and down the room we went, Goliath flailing the broom with telling effect on nothing except the lamps and the furniture. With one mighty swish of the broom a lamp topped over; with another, a vase; and a blow aimed at young David zooming up a curtain knocked off a wooden cornice which fell with a terrible clatter across a delicate antique tilt-top table, neatly shearing off an edge.

Early in the contest I had opened the door to the terrace and had propped the screen back. I had wanted to give my opponent every chance to leave the combat honorably. But I had apparently not reckoned with the honor of the tribe of flying squirrels. At no time did this one show any evidence of desiring to give up the fray short complete annihilation of the enemy.

About one o'clock, however, the squirrel decided upon new strategy; so he sped to the fireplace, scrambled over neatly stacked firewood and pinecones, and disappeared into the chimney. By this time I was the next thing to a raging maniac and my living room was a shambles. But I welcomed respite.

Worn and weak I sank into a chair to think. As I sat, I devised a diabolic scheme that I hoped might win the battle. Congratulating myself on my cleverness, I rounded up a little dead-fall rat trap, baited it with the meat of one of the left-over Christmas pecans, and put the infernal machine on the hearth. Having done so, I turned off the lights and went to my room, where I partially undressed and lay down on the bed.

For an exasperatingly long time nothing happened. Then bang! the trap went off. Into the living room I rushed and switched on the lights. The trap had been sprung and the nut meat was gone, but no squirrel was in sight. Not to be outdone I repeated the experiment; once, twice, three times. On the fourth baiting I was successful. When I dashed into the room, there was my little friend out cold, his head firmly clamped down by the wire arm of the trap, his legs stretched, and his furry web exposed.

"You look adequately immobilized," I said, "but I'm not taking any chances on your still being able to scratch and claw. You'll stay right where you are until morning."

Back to bed I went in triumph. But as I reached up to turn off the light that had almost been rendered unnecessary by the first dawn, a sudden wave of conscience swept over me.

"The creature may be suffering," I thought. "Maybe I ought either to have set him free outside or to have put him completely out of pain with a quick hammer-blow on the head." And a vision of my friend, Anita Van Fleet, the smart, crusading president of the local S.P.C.A. rose up to accuse me. Anita had had the sheriff on people for less.

"Oh, damn!" I said, jerking the light cord with callous finality.

The sleep of the unjust was descending like delightful, tepid waves of mist when a clatter, clatter, clatter came once again from the living room. Clatter, clatter, clatter. The beast was plainly walking away with the trap!

Dead tired and half asleep, I made a final trip to the living room; and with absolutely no feeling for the sensibilities of animal life, I grabbed the battered broom and swept the squirrel, trap and all, out the door. Wrapped in a steamer rug, I spent what was left of the traditional sleeping hours on the divan, now athwart the cluttered living room floor. I did not realize where I was until I became conscious of the ringing of an alarm clock somewhere in the detestable distance.

My first vicious urge was to view the frozen corpse of my late visitor so justly assigned, trap attached, to a frigid fate on the terrace. When I opened the door, the trap was there all right, but the squirrel was not. Looking up quickly, I saw the saucy flash of a brown tail among the bluish gray limbs of a bare, icy tree.

On my way to work, only the strongest resolution kept me from marching into a newspaper office and irritably planking down a dollar or some such amount for a brief ad to be inserted the next day in a column headed "For Sale — Real Estate."

Dr. Hartley, long-time head of the English Department at North Carolina State University, is a nationally-known author and critic, who, lest his humor be taken too seriously, does not dislike animals.

THE ELM

No one, I think,
However much
He loves a tree,
Can love an elm.
The elm is a proliferate
And a trespasser.
It is not enough
That its lower branches
Grow downward, vexing mowers;
It is a creator of disorder,
Scattering seeds
So that elm shoots grow
In basement window wells,
In crevices in walks,
Parasitically in japonicas,
Among the azaleas,
The wisterias, nandinas,
The forsythias
And pyracanthas.
And elm shoots
Aren't easily pulled up.

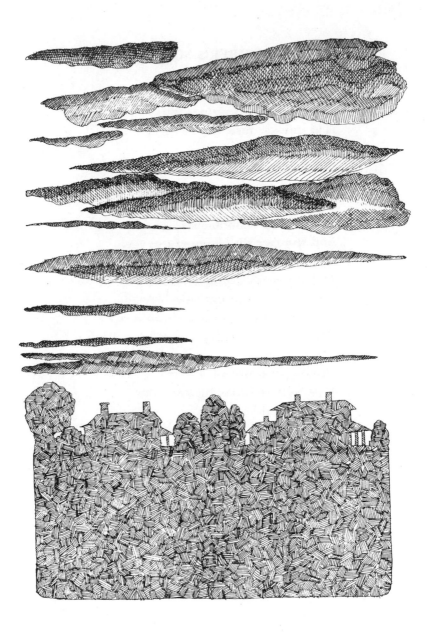

SEPTEMBER'S SONG

The seasons in their cycle run
Quickly out of summer into fall
And quickly now the changes
      come,
Bringing summer's freedoms to
      an end.
Now the way turns back again
      to school,
And summer's pleasure places
      close,
And summer's crops are taken in.
For this is now September's reign,
The time of the autumnal equinox,
And soon, before September's
      gone,
Cooling weather will foretell
Another year is racing into time.

REQUIESCAT AT GETTYSBURG

Beneath the trees overlooking
      the rolling battleground
And the quiet fields where so
      many men died by stone walls
      and rail fences.
A bronze monument stands and
      with it a memorial bearing
      chiseled imperishably on its
      face the tribute:
"To the eternal glory of North
      Carolina's soldiers
Who on this battlefield displayed
      heroism unsurpassed,
Sacrificing all in support of their
      cause. . . "
And below the tribute is the
      reminder
That at Gettysburg July 1,2 and
      3 in 1863
One of every four of the 30
      thousand Confederate casualties
Was a North Carolinian.
And not only at Gettysburg did
      North Carolinians show the
      way to die.
"First at Bethel, farthest at
      Gettysburg, last at
      Appomattox,"
From the onset to the end, North
      Carolina blood flowed in a
      pointless war.

And in all the fighting since
           brave men have died for causes
That new wars make obsolete
           and history obscures.
And the valor of the dead lives on
           only on the monuments
Of wars all fought in vain.

DEATH OF A HOUSE

How quickly the wreckers
Smashed the slate shingles from
      the roof
And broke away the rafters.
How long had the old house stood
Secure under its slate roof
With its seasoned siding
And its tall gables with
      scrollwork?
The craftsmen who built it had
      built well.
From the large circular window in
      the gable
Overlooking the front entrance
To the graceful millwork
      decorating the upper story,
There was an archaic charm
      about the house
And a sturdiness and substance.
How quickly the wreckers
Broke the circular window from
      its frame
And knocked away the siding.
Broken glass and shattered boards
Lie now in a shambles about
      its foundations
And the strong old house,
      the graceful house,
Is now a roofless facade.
How quickly the wreckers

Obliterate the craftsmen's work.
How soon the city will forget
How it was before the wreckers came.

THE QUESTION?

I noticed for the first time
 as I sat on the patio
late on a mid-September afternoon
 clusters of red berries on
 the dogwood trees.
And I remembered the white
 blossoms
which adorned the trees
 in April.
Which, I wondered, had the greater
 beauty?
I did not know.
Nor did I know how old
 the berries were,
Or how long they would last.
I knew only that in April
There would be blossoms again
And that when they came I
 would rejoice.
And I would wonder then:
Which is the greater miracle,
The beginning of life's cycle
 or its fruition?

SOMETHING, JUST ANYTHING
IF YOU'RE REALLY IN NEED

What is this poverty they talk about when they talk of rural needs and urban slums? It is not merely something to be lamented by sociologists and to provide projects for the North Carolina Fund and the Office of Economic Opportunity. It is people weary and wanting, and it can be a hungry somebody as close as your own back door.

She stood there, on the steps before the screen door to the back porch, clutching in one hand a dirty shopping bag filled, it seemed, with rags and leaning with the other on an old umbrella.

"Do you," she asked, "be needing anybody for washing windows or anything? I is looking for something to do to get something to eat."

We have a girl who comes in, she was told. We really don't need anybody else.

"If you could let me have a quarter," she suggested, "that would help me out."

The headlines in the paper only a few days before had reported the cost of living in this nation of affluence had climbed to an all-time high. Across the street the neighbors had just bought a new piano. Next door a family with a son in college had two cars parked in their driveway. Nobody was well-off but neither were any in need. It was spring in an affluent America, and now at the backdoor a hungry woman wanted work or 25 cents.

How did you happen to come here? the woman was asked. Did somebody tell you someone on this street needed help?

"I just came looking," she answered. "Nobody told me to. I just felt like somebody here-abouts might have something and I been near about everywhere else."

It was evening weeks earlier when the other caller came. He, too, carried a bag and walked with an improvised cane, and he looked as though he had been out-fitted at a rummage sale.

"Have you got any work you want done?" he asked.

There was no work.

"Just anything would help," he said. "If you got some old clothes, maybe some old shoes, or something I could sell to get something to eat."

There were some old shoes and he took them along with two over-size cans of pork and beans.

"I sure do thank you," he said. "I sure do."

But weren't you around here before? he was challenged. You aren't making a habit of this are you? There must be other streets in a city this size. Why don't you go visiting some of them?

"I just happened to come this way," he answered. "The gentleman up the ways, he said for me to come back and he'd see if he couldn't have something for me."

But if you go to the same well too often, he was told, people are going to get the idea you're a bum.

"But that's what I am." he said grinning. "I am a bum. That's what I have to be. Unless I can get a little something to do,"

Down the street, a neighbor coming home from work drove his new car into his garage. A few hundred feet away children on new bicycles and skates played on the large paved parking area serving the carport of a long, low ranch-house. A few hundred yards up the street, workmen finishing a new recreation room piled into their truck to leave for the night.

It wasn't an affluent neighborhood. None of its residents would call themselves well-to-do. None of them could really believe the man with the grin and the bag really had to beg to eat.

Driving home from downtown to the suburbs, the people on the street would pass the ill-kept houses in which people like the man with the bag live.

"You know," the neighbor said, "if they had any self-respect they wouldn't live like that. There are some people who wouldn't know what to do with it if they had anything."

The women came in their station wagons early nearly every Saturday morning, hauling loads of out-grown and out-of-fashion clothing to sell in the parking lot of the big state office building, to raise money for their churches and clubs. Some of them sold for themselves.

"How much is them shoes?" the customers would ask. "I couldn't give no more than 10 cents. That's all the other ladies ever ask."

"Has you got any men's pants? I told myself before I came this morning I was going to buy my boy some pants if there was any to get."

"They've got money," the women would tell each other. "They've got money; they say they don't but they have."

The children were roller skating when the woman in the molting fur coat came.

"I bet some of the things those childrens has done with would just fit my grandchildrens," she said. "Just anything would be nice, just anything."

When the knocking sounded at the door, the man raised his head from his paper. His wife would see who it was. A few moments later the wife came into the den looking curiously frightened.

"Would you see what that man wants?" she asked her

155

husband. "He looks sick or perhaps he's drunk."

"Would you take me home?" the stranger asked half in tears and half in challenge.

"Home?" the man demanded. "Home! Where in the heck do you live?" The stranger said he lived on the other side of the city, at least eight or more miles away.

He was a white man. He was dirty, hollow-eyed and he was drunk.

"Would you take me home?" he pleaded. "I'm a good man. I own property . . . I can show you my house . . . I'm somebody . . ."

He staggered.

"I don't have to go begging . . . I can show you my house."

And the man with the bag, and the woman with the umbrella, and the woman in the molting fur coat, they had nothing to show. They had no pride to lose.

And as the neighbor had remarked, and as the stranger might have remarked, when he was sober, if you give some people something they wouldn't know what to do with it.

June 1968

R.F.D. PLUS – SOMETHING
MORE THAN A MAILBOX

The one-horse plow and the old iron pump haven't vanished from the countryside. Dozens can be seen across rural North Carolina today supporting mailboxes.

They serve, as do other relics of the rural scene put to similar use, to link the state's agricultural past with its suburban present.

People have been expressing their individuality, creativity and imagination in mailboxes and stanchions for as long as Americans have had rural free delivery.

In the early days, some R.F.D. patrons expressed themselves with considerably less restraint than is now permitted. Just about anything that could be nailed to a fence or set on a post was used, and rural carriers making their rounds often had to leave mail in old lard cans, cigar boxes, drainage pipes, soap boxes (in the days of wooden boxes) or whatever else the patron cared to erect.

The Post Office Department soon realized things were getting out of hand. Government standards were adopted and mailboxes had to be approved. If a box was too unsuitable, the carrier could refuse to recognize it as a stop.

Even so, individualists were undaunted. There were always ways to get around regulations and to beat the standards. You have only to look from your car as you drive along country roads and through suburban areas to see examples of the many ways a mailbox can be made to look like something else.

You'll see mailboxes that look like miniatures of the houses before which they stand and mailboxes that look like barrels, or log cabins, or birdhouses, or covered wagons. You'll see mailboxes in bowers, or with ivy climbing about their supports, or set on trelliswork with roses blooming in season, or primly held erect on a section of pipe, or resting indifferently on the tops of old oil drums.

And wagon wheels. They are often used, with mailboxes spaced around their circumferences and with a post and axle through their hubs, so the carrier can turn the wheel to reach each box in turn. Old auto wheels and even bicycle wheels sometimes serve in a like manner.

When R.F.D. was begun Oct. 1, 1896, it was largely a service for farmers. Today's route carriers serve fewer farmers but many more Americans of all interests and classes. During the past three decades, the number of patrons receiving rural delivery has increased 40 percent, and the 30,981 rural mailmen across the nation travel approximately 2 million miles a day making deliveries to more than 36 million patrons.

Old plows and pumps, and wagon wheels, tell how it used to be but they are too often found along R.F.D. routes to be favored now by the true individualist. He has attempted to be different by using forged sections of heavy chain in place of posts, or by fixing brackets to old guns. And here and there he has erected his box on the outstretched arms of a cut-out of Uncle Sam gaily painted red, white and blue.

There are many ways to mount a mailbox and to disguise one, and if you'll watch as you drive you'll see nearly every idea somewhere along the road.

THE VIOLETS

On a knoll at the far edge of the tobacco field, a small grove of tall cedars stood sentinel. As you walked from the farmhouse towards them, you could see the remains of an old iron fence. When you reached the fence, you could see the tombstones and markers over which the cedars watched.

Once every homeplace had such quiet groves, and in them, chiseled on the tombstones, were the names of your forebears.

Older members of your family would tell you stories about the family graveyard. How your grandfather's grandfather had hidden swords and guns beneath a coffin in one of the graves when the Yankees came through. How there was supposed to be an iron chest full of silverware buried during the war and for some reason never dug up.

As a child you would climb over the iron fence, read the inscriptions and gather violets that curiously seemed always to flourish there.

If you were to return to the old homeplace now, you well might find all traces of the old cemetery obliterated. As farms changed hands, and farmlands became housing developments, or golf courses, or underwent the other changes that have taken place in rural areas since World War II, the family cemetery had largely disappeared. Those which have not vanished have been overrun with briars and honeysuckle. Only here and there in North Carolina now can be found family graveyards with fences and stones still intact and families which still keep them in the old tradition.

The story of the vanishing family graveyards is also the

161

story of many other things which once were familiar across North Carolina.

The old log tobacco curing barns with tepees of split logs for their kilns, the old wells with their little A roofs and one bucket which went down when the other was pulled up, the "dairies" where milk and butter were kept cool and other perishables were stored, and of course the old privies; they all have largely vanished.

With them have gone the little stores which farmers kept for the convenience of themselves, tenants, field hands and neighbors; the little plank churches, the old frame schoolhouses, the depots by the railroad tracks and the small post offices which often stood nearby.

You find them occasionally as you travel along the backroads: the old stores with fading and rusting signs; the old post offices with lettering so weather-worn you barely can make out "U.S. Post Office" and the name of the place; the old school and church buildings sagging and with windows gone, serving sometimes for the storage of feed, fertilizer or farm equipment which has largely gone to rust, or empty of all except old memories.

And such memories — different for each of us.

Remember how you would go with your father to the post office near the depot and wait with others like yourselves for the train which brought the mail?

And how, after the postmaster (or in many cases, the postmistress) had sorted out the contents of the mail sack, you would wish there had been a package for your house? Mamma had ordered things from the mail order catalogue. Hopefully the next mail would bring them.

If you were school age in the twenties and thirties, you will remember how on Saturdays everybody gathered at the two or three stores in what was called "town." The stores carried everything from groceries to clothing, from kerosene to farm supplies. Many had a porch across the front where your elders would sit and talk while you wondered whether to spend your nickel on the big Pepsi or the big orange from the drink box — or the biggest nickel candy bar.

The barns were as much a part of your life as keeping the woodbox filled for your mother and going to Sunday school at the old white clapboard church.

You would help clean the stalls in the barns where the family's cows spent the nights, driving the cows out in the morning after milking and driving back from the pasture at dusk. And you would put feed in the troughs for the mules and play in the hay in the loft.

When the tobacco was ready to come out of the field, you would take your turn at night keeping the fires going in the kilns of the old log, clay-chinked curing barns, and listen while somebody older, who knew about such things, would tell about the first World War or some tall story about hunting or ghosts to keep himself and you awake.

The old barns, like the old family graveyards, are now in a way ghosts themselves.

They are symbols of our past, but the life they represented shaped for many of us our futures. For in North Carolina today, there are many lawyers, doctors, journalists, educators and business leaders who might never have strived so hard to get to and through college if they had not been so anxious to escape the toil and economic uncertainty that in their boyhood, in the era of the hoe and the mule, was the lot of the farmer.

They have escaped. But they have not forgotten. The memories of their boyhood grow fonder as the years mellow them, and they wish they could go back. And they wonder if the violets would be there if they did.

CONVERSATION PIECE

Don't fume if the person at the head of the line tries to start a conversation with the sales clerk. It could be you.

The saleslady reached for the ball point pens.

"Any color will be all right," the woman told her.

"No, let me have a green one. I've got so many black ones. It will be easier to tell them apart.

"I lent my pen to my son and he lost it. When I got after him he said, 'Mother, it only cost 25 cents.' It cost a dollar, I told him a dollar."

She rummaged in her purse and drew out a dollar. The saleslady still held the pen and waited. A man waiting behind the woman moved out to lean against the counter.

"He said," the woman went on, 'Well, I thought it was 25 cents.' But it wasn't, I told him. It was a dollar. A dollar and four cents with tax."

The saleslady waited, listening indifferently, and let the woman talk on.

The woman talked, hungering for conversation. She talked the way people used to be able to talk to their neighbors before people living side by side became strangers. She talked the way people would talk in their homes before families became scattered and home became a place where only the elderly and those too small or infirm to go on their own are found except at night.

She talked as if she had no one else to talk to, except the son and then only when her words could catch him on the fly. She was all the lonesome and forgotten people who, while the world rushed, are left unnoticed, unneeded and unheard.

"I like black pens but I have too many," she said, "Green's a good color. At least it's different. I don't think I'll let him borrow this one. I got some aspirin here but I want to bring them back. Ballpoints are all right. I like the other kind but they're all right. I like green."

The man looked at the saleslady and shook his head. The woman had more to say.

"I guess I take a lot of aspirin."

"A dollar four," the saleslady said.

"Oh, yes," the woman said. She sounded as though she suddenly had become conscious of her surroundings.

"A dollar four, did you say?"

"A dollar four."

The woman reached again into her purse. "Green," she said. "I like that green all right."

The man was becoming impatient.

The woman handed her money to the saleslady.

"I won't let him borrow this one," she said.

"Maybe if you let him buy his own pen," the saleslady said politely and yet with a tone of dismissal, "that might teach him to be more careful."

The woman laughed faintly. "Of course," she said, taking the green pen, and closed her purse.

"It's such a nice day, I think, don't you. It really is nice."

She turned away clasping her purse and her purchase.

The man, obviously impatient now, spoke quickly to the saleslady, as though he expected the woman to turn back.

"Guess she doesn't have anybody much to talk to," he said.

"Guess she doesn't," the saleslady agreed.

The man made his purchase.

"Guess you have a lot of people come in who want a chance to talk to somebody, lonesome people, I mean."

The saleslady rang up the sale.

"That's a fact," she said emphatically.

And to the man who had a few more things to say, it sounded as though she was saying he already had said enough.

BRIGHTEN THE CORNER WHERE YOU ARE

When I was a child, my Sunday school class used to sing "Brighten the Corner Where You Are." I've forgotten the rest of the words. When I read about ecology, the environment and pollution, I wonder if everybody else hasn't forgotten, too.

Pollution is a people problem. It won't be solved until all of us realize it is.

Blocking the construction of dams, reservoirs and power plants makes headlines, but no real headway will be made towards our ecological goals until each of us does more to brighten the corner where we are.

Granted the conservationists are right, it is illogical to deny people the benefits of flood control and water supply projects and reasonably priced utility service in the name of conservation while the most obvious desecration of the environment continues unchecked.

The incongruity of it all confronts you whereever you live, along every street and road you travel, because all of us everywhere are living with and contributing to pollution; and the Conservation Crusade will succeed only if we deal first with the pollution we create as individuals and permit in our communities.

Think of what could be accomplished if everyone cleared his property of abandoned cars, appliances, and the other junk we all allow to accumulate. Imagine how much pollution could be eliminated if we would teach our children not to discard candy wrappers, cartons, drink cups, cans and bottles wherever they happen to finish consuming the contents — and would practice what we teach.

Imagine, too, how much better our environment would

be if we insisted our local and state governments adopt and rigorously enforce anti-litter and anti-dumping laws. And by united action as consumers we could force manufacturers to end the wasteful annual model changes and built-in obsolescence responsible for much of our junk and compel processors to reduce the packaging which adds to the cost of everything we buy and generates tons of waste paper, aluminum and plastic.

We are burying ourselves in our own wastes. We, not the dam builders, the utilities industry nor the other popular targets of ecological exasperation, are thoughtlessly the major culprits. If we really want to brighten our environment, we've got to start with ourselves.

THE WILD PLUMS

Only yesterday,
Well past the time they should
    have bloomed,
I realized the wild plums had not
    bloomed this year.
There were other blossoms
But there were none of these
That so long had been a challenge
    to my ire.
I had fought the wild plum with
    axe and pick;
I had cut away each shoot above
    the ground,
And each spring there it would be
    again,
Showing its blossoms,
Telling me it had survived.
Can it be then that at last I have
    won
The fight to keep it and the bram-
    bles and the vines
From over-running the thin lawn
    among the pines?
Is it really dead
And all its blossoms, too?
Or is it dormant in its root,
Waiting for another spring and
    my regrets?
I have won the battle, and I have
    lost.

JUANITA

The girl I almost married
Turned as I passed
And spoke to a tall youth.
Was he her son?
He answered like a son
Replying to his mother.
I spoke her name, and she mine
And hurried on my way.
Looking back, I saw them
Walking together,
The girl I almost married
And the tall youth,
And I reflected on what might have been
And hurried on, home-bound
To the girl I married
And my children.

GET RID OF IT WHILE YOU CAN

That old washing machine, the old refrigerator you've been keeping in the garage; get rid of them before it's too late.

One day before long you may find you can't.

"You can't sell 'em for junk," the owner of a Raleigh furniture and appliance store said. "The junk dealers don't want them. You can't put 'em in the city dump because when they rust out they collapse and the fills cave in."

The furniture store proprietor was talking about the old appliances he and other dealers take as trade-ins. He had several sitting behind his store waiting to be carried off and with no place to take them.

"But you can always salvage parts off them," a friend suggested. "You can salvage the electric motors and maybe use the eyes off the old electric ranges for repairs."

"It doesn't work out that way," the dealer replied. "The motor you save isn't the one you need, and you accumulate a lot of motors and parts and stove eyes that finally get in the way.

"It's a problem. You can't sell the stuff as junk and there's no place to dump it."

An appliance dealer up the street agreed. "I don't know what we're going to do," he said, "unless we go out in the country somewhere and buy us an acre of land to use as a dump and bury the things."

Even before the junkyards stopped buying it, junk made up of old appliances brought only a penny a pound.

"Old appliances with porcelain finishes are like bathtubs," a junk dealer explained. "They're hard to scrap. The porcelain has to be burned off. You pour gasoline on

171

them and set them afire and then spray water on them while they're still hot so the porcelain will crack off. It's a lot of trouble."

Dealers in cities like Raleigh generally don't like to bother with appliance trade-ins but they find people like the illusion of getting an allowance for trade-ins when they buy. So long as people like to kid themselves or be kidded, dealers will continue to trade, even though both they and the customer might come out as well or better on straight sales.

Just picking up an old appliance and carting it to the store costs a dealer in time and labor. Then, if he has to keep the trade-in on hand, there's also the expense of storage space.

It's becoming the same way with old cars. In a few years more, you won't be able to give them away. You may even have to pay to get rid of them.

So there it is. And there is that old refrigerator. Get it out while the getting's good.

This affluent nation's assembly line is ceaseless. Appliances, autos, bathtubs and gadgets, they're coming off in a flood. And the cemeteries for the discards are filled.

December 1970

TWO WAYS IN SUMMER

Now is the time when all
    outdoors
Beckons and our fancies speak
To turn us from the chores we
    have to do
And set us dreaming at our work
Of the pleasures of vacationtime.
Now is the time when mountains
    rise
With all the grandeur of their
    breathless views
And cast their spell across our
    restive days,
And the seacoast with its rolling
    surf,
Ebbing, flowing, washing on the
    sand,
Pulls against the mountains'
    strength;
And we would go two ways at
    once in joy.
And in another summer of
    delight,
Between the mountains and the
    coast,
Give ourselves again
Insouciantly to summer's spell.

A BED FOR HISTORY

There are still in North Carolina grandmothers — and grandfathers too — whose mothers and fathers told them stories of how it used to be during the Civil War. Among the happiest pleasures of their mellowing years is telling and retelling what they were told, and one of the happiest heritages of their grandchildren will be the pleasure their grandparents would draw from theirs when they would enjoy the old tales together.

The next time we go to Warrenton, Grandmother said, I want you to ask Cousin Mary to show you the bed Robert E. Lee's daughter's died in, Cat.

Really, the little girl laughed. Oh when will we go?

One Sunday real soon, Grandmother replied. And when we get there you be sure to ask Cousin Mary what I told you.

The child marvelled at it. How long ago Robert E. Lee had lived, she thought. She had studied about him in school. His time, she knew, was way back in the Civil War years, so far back that even Sweet Mama, Grandmother's mother, had not been born then, and now here was Nannie telling her that somebody living now, a cousin in Warrenton, had a connection with his daughter and, even more miraculous, the miraculous bed.

Is it a real bed? she asked Grandmother.

Oh it is, Grandmother assured her. A bed like those they had in those days, a very nice bed.

Did it have posters and a canopy and everything? the child asked.

Well now I don't know that it had a canopy,

Grandmother said. Fact is, I don't believe it did.

Was it real little? asked the child.

Oh no, Grandmother said with a laugh; she was enjoying the child's enthusiastic curiosity. Oh no, it was a regular size bed.

And Cousin Mary has it? Can people sleep in it? Do they sleep in it now?

Oh I can't tell you all that, Grandmother said smiling. You'll just have to wait till we get there. Cousin Mary will show you. She knows the whole history of it.

There was almost nothing about history that Grandmother did know so long as it dealt with the Civil War. She was best though at things that happened in or were related to Vance and Warren counties. And nearly everything she knew could be related to her family — which was only natural; nearly everybody in Vance and Warren was related to everybody else. Nearly everybody in the old families were cousins.

Not far from her home dozens of Civil War soldiers were buried, and once a year there is a ceremony at the little cemetery. Grandmother as one of the UDC ladies, always had a part in arranging the ceremonies and getting the cemetery prepared for them. Cedars now grew among the graves and only a few days ago, the man who worked for Grandmother and Grandfather and lived in their backyard, had gone, at their request, to dig up the stumps of cedars that had died. Grandfather had had him pack the roots and wood into cardboard boxes so that the little girl's parents could take it back to Raleigh to use in their fireplace.

Grandmother had a list of the names of all the soldiers in the cemetery, and she had clippings and papers telling not only about the cemetery (the only Confederate cemetery in Vance County, she proudly would note), but also about the Confederate hospital at which the soldiers

175

had been patients during the Civil War.

The hand of history lay heavily everywhere and, as Grandmother liked to relate it to her grandchildren, it was as close to her and them as the many cousins she would name.

But what Grandmother was telling about now was new to the child. It was, the little girl felt, most unusual. It was a thing which more than anything else she had heard, either from Grandmother or in her classes at school, which brought the Civil War alive for her.

But, Grandmother, the child asked, why did the bed have to be so big?

It wasn't big, Grandmother answered. It was just the regular size.

That's what I mean, the child said. Why did it have to be the regular size? Why would a cat need a bed that big?

A cat, darling? Grandmother asked, unsure that she had heard correctly.

Yes, a cat, the child said. Robert E. Lee's daughter's cat. The cat that died.

Oh, darling, I didn't say anything about a cat. Perhaps I said your name, Catherine, but I didn't say anything about a cat. I was telling you about General Lee's daughter.

And not a cat, the child said. Not a cat that had a bed that it died in.

My goodness, Grandmother said laughing. Whatever gave you that idea?

And the child felt there was nothing now that she wanted to see.

All there was, she told herself, was just another bed.

You just wait till we go to Warrenton, Grandmother said brightly, then Cousin Mary will tell you all about it.

But the child wasn't sure now that she even wanted to go.

THE LAST TULIP

All the other tulips I know have
Given up their petals and retired
To give attention to their annual
    chore
Of growing new bulbs for another
    spring.
And you, discordant plant,
Here you are still bearing
A crimson cup one might call a
    crown,
Defiant in the row alone,
Nodding to the stirring breeze,
With such pretty graces and such
    airs.
A cheat you are and something
    of a flirt.
But I know your bravado will
    not last
But another day or two and then
You too will call the season to
    an end.

FAIREST OCTOBER

When woodlands show so many
    shades of gold
And leaves red and russet scurry
    in the wind,
October brings its beauty to us
    all.
When whiter clouds roam bluer
    skies
And brooks run with their purest
    streams
And mountains reach their color
    heights,
October writes a poem with its
    moods.
Fairest month, running a full
    range
Of the best that of all the others
    bring,
October is the season's pause, the
    final treat,
A second taste of summer's
    warmth
Mixed with winter's tang; a
    second chorus
That is ours to sing
Before winter sings the earth to
    sleep.

REQUIEM FOR A CITY

There must be change if there is to be growth. There must be in growing cities a kaleidoscope of ever changing patterns, of old buildings being torn down and new buildings rising, of old landmarks giving way for progress. Still, there is something in all of us that is called nostalgia, and it warms our memories and it sometimes makes what was more substantial than what is and what will be.

It isn't there now. There is nothing now except a barricade enclosing a construction site.

Almost since yesterday it seems, the city has changed. The Raleigh of buildings so familiar that they still linger in the mind's eye has become a Raleigh tearing down and putting up. Yet not until you look closely or unless you have been away, and are looking anew, do you realize how much is different.

Not unless you tried to remember what stood where the angular orange steel skeletons stand, where the new buildings rise, and what there used to be where the gaps show between the storefronts would you remember they had not been there always.

Not unless you try to picture it do you realize the picture has disappeared.

The candy store on Fayetteville Street is gone. The alley leading to a court unchanged for 50 years now is a driveway for a parking lot.

The clock repair shop behind the old City Hall. Wasn't it only a few weeks ago that you'd seen the German clock in a jar ticking in its window?

The deep hole being dug deeper back in the barricade.

What had been there and what will there be when the digging was finished?

The old granite Wake County Courthouse is gone. You and crowds of others watched over the weeks as it was demolished by a crane swinging a mammoth ball, battering down first the central section and then the two ends. A proud new courthouse now occupies its place.

Somebody you knew had lived in a house on the site of the new State House. Where was it that the house stood? And what was it that you used to notice and had meant to ask about in the house among the houses razed on Edenton Street?

On the corner of Martin and Salisbury streets, the new First Federal Savings Building now stands where the old Academy Building used to be. There were shops along the Martin Street side. Or were there?

On the corner of Fayetteville and Davie Streets, where the tall new BB&T office building now stands, that's where the old City Hall was. Hadn't there been some stores or offices or both between it and Hudson-Belk? Wasn't there a filling station behind it?

On Wilmington Street, where the Job P. Wyatt hardware store was before it moved to the northern end of Downtown Boulevard, when was it that part of it became Wyatt-Quarles Seed Company and the other part an annex to Hudson-Belk? Where was it along there that you used to find the Carolina Hardware Company? Or was it farther up the street?

On West Martin Street, the sturdy building in which Josephus Daniels edited *The News and Observer* is gone and now the parking lot laid over its foundations has become a loading ramp and annex for the paper's circulation department. Didn't the old newspaper office have marble steps and a revolving door? How long had it been gone?

Five years? Ten? Fifteen? Can it be that long?

And on Wilmington Street there was an old livery stable. Or was it out farther?

And a church stood about there or some place along there.

If you close your eyes and think you can picture it all, the windows with stained glass, the entrance on the corner.

It was there. Or it might have been. Only everything looks different now.

Or perhaps your memory deceives you.

Or perhaps it never was.

WHEN BLOSSOMS FALL

Yesterday the apple trees were
    white;
Only yesterday their fragile
    blossoms bloomed,
Accenting the green pines
    behind them as
Jonquils had not long before.
And now the apple boughs
    are green
And leaves grow in such
    profusion that
None can tell there had been
    blossoms there.
And so it is that blossoms go,
Petals falling like the rains
    of spring;
To be forgotten, until
New growth will bring
More blossoms for another spring.

PARTNER TO A MIRACLE

The biggest tomato, the longest sweet potato, the night blooming cereus showing its blossoms; how does your garden grow?

Whether it grows on a farm or a backyard or in nothing bigger than a flower box, it grows in an undeclared sweepstakes of superlatives in which the extraordinary is as exciting among green thumbs as the biggest fish is among anglers.

Every summer when the tomatoes ripen, somebody you know, and perhaps even you, will bring forth a tomato nearly as big as a cantaloupe. Every week in season a double bloom will be discovered where there should be only one.

Mention watermelons and you'll learn somebody in your own county had one so large he had to ask his wife to help him bring it to the house.

And there's always the night blooming cereus. That's one of the several kinds of cactus plants with large, white flowers that open at night. There must be a couple of dozen of them around Raleigh. Every time one of them blooms somebody discovers anew that here in his own yard is one of nature's miracles.

The headlines, the radio bulletins and the television newscasts, they come at you every morning reporting new disasters and dilemmas and all the other things that happen to people and people cause and people do to others.

And the man with the biggest tomato, the longest sweet potato or the night blooming cereus takes it all in, knowing that he — here in North Carolina, with his own hands and the help of those immutable laws greater than any man has written — has been a party to something bigger and better than he ever could have managed alone.

YOU'VE GOT TO BE AN ACTIVIST TOO

One way you can tell you're growing stodgy is your attitude toward change.

It unsettles you. It disturbs your complacency, and you find yourself resenting it and the expressions of it — so much so that if Santa's elves turned out with placards in Fayetteville Street, you'd probably sick Spiro Agnew on 'em.

And the word *activist* raises your blood pressure.

Granted there have been too many protest marches and demonstrations, granted they're self-defeating, America needs activists.

It needs them in its communities and its organizations.

Think what a healthy thing it would be for North Carolina if every one of us became an activist for constructive causes.

We could make all of our communities better places for all the people in them. We could make our organizations dynamic agencies for meeting people's needs.

All it would take would be for somebody like you to make the first move. If you want to get things done your way, that's what you must do. In doing so, you'll show that good citizens can be as dedicated and determined as those who, to your way of thinking, want to wreck the country.

So if you have ideas for improving your community, put your ideas to work. If you feel it should have a water system or a sewer system, or some other service or facility, start talking, acting and organizing. That's how North Carolina's EMCs were started. That's how many other needs were met.

When your co-op, Farm Bureau, Grange, church and club hold meetings you should attend, make sure you're there — not just to win door prizes but to take a knowledgeable part in the proceedings. By doing so you'll help make sure every organization to which you belong is a moving force for the best interests of all its members.

Remember, it's your community, your local government, your co-op, your organization, your church. If you want it run right, you must be active in it.

Stick your neck out. Be an activist for something constructive. That's the only way you can defuse the demonstrators and make this the kind of country everybody wants.

STRANGER AT THE DOOR

By Edward E. Brown, Jr.

He had seemed like a clean-cut young chap with good intentions. He said he was a student at a nearby university and represented some company I had never heard of.

"I am looking for families to be used in my company's advertising," he explained. "I must choose one family — only one family — from this area." He stressed the "one" and added we would be paid if we were the family chosen.

"Just what is your company's product?" I asked. I was surprised when he said he represented a well-known encyclopedia company. In fact, I thought the company name was a little misleading. But the young man was very articulate and smooth.

He had come to the door empty handed. So I naturally didn't suspect his intentions. Salesmen usually have a briefcase or something, you know. But now he wanted to go to his car and get one of his encyclopedias, but not for us to buy, you understand.

"Let me get one of the books for you to examine," he said. "I want to see your reaction and you must decide if you could really write a letter telling how good you think the books are."

"Just a minute," I said. "You'd better tell us what's in it for us, or you might be wasting your time."

"You get a free set of encyclopedias," he said, and rushed out to get a sample book.

That sounded pretty good to me. I had taken a few advertising courses in college. I knew that some companies use testimonials to promote their products. And even though I wasn't Jack Benny or Arnold Palmer, I had seen some pretty ordinary people on TV endorsing anything from chewing tobacco to cake mixes.

By now he was back and handed the book to us for our scrutiny. He must have spent at least 20 minutes acclaiming the myriad qualities of the book we held in our hands. Water wouldn't hurt it. You could hold the entire book up with one page and it wouldn't tear out. And on and on.

"Now could you in good conscience endorse these encyclopedias?" he asked. By that time I was sure there was none better anywhere.

My wife and I looked at each other and nodded affirmatively in agreement.

"Yes," we said in chorus.

"Are you sure now?" he asked.

"Yes," we said again even more sure this time.

I was beginning to feel a little uncomfortable. The books were good all right. He didn't even have to sell me on them. Most all colleges had them in their libraries so I knew they were good. I felt greedy sitting there nodding my head trying to be convincing so we would be the "one" chosen family.

"Good!" he said. "And since you are the family I have chosen, I'm going to give you a chance to buy our 10-volume set of children's short stories at a special price."

My faith in our Santa Claus visitor sagged. He was talking about money now. And after all, our little girl was only two feet long and five months old.

Another 15 minutes expounding on the merits of the junior books, we were quoted a good price on them. And we really didn't have to buy them anyway.

By now we were sure of one thing; we wanted to be an "advertising family" and receive the free set of encyclopedias. And, yes, I decided to buy the junior books, too. Figured I would read them to the baby so she would be quoting them by the time she could talk.

"Fine!" he said. "Now there are certain conditions you must agree to. First, you must agree to buy the yearly supplement encyclopedias for the next ten years. You'll, of course, get these at a special discount price."

That's not unreasonable I thought. After all, I'd probably buy them anyway to keep my set updated.

"Secondly," he said, "you must join our research club for the next ten years. Your membership will entitle you to write in and ask any question you might have. We have a staff of 300 experts who are available to give you full answers."

"But that's what I want the encyclopedias for," I protested mildly. "I can do my own research. And, besides, I just finished school and I hope I'm through researching for awhile."

"But suppose you had to give a speech," he pointed out. "You could simply send your subject in and receive a fully researched speech already prepared for you."

Although reluctantly, I agreed I might be able to use the research service. Of course, I also realized that this meant more money. I was beginning to seriously doubt this guy's intentions. But to receive a set of encyclopedias valued at over $500 "free" wasn't anything to snear at.

About this time some friends dropped in so I told the young man to figure out the total costs for the junior books, the annual supplements, and the research membership.

Everyone was talking at one time and there was a lot of confusion. But not so much that I noticed the total bill he handed me amounted to over $400. The "free" set of encyclopedias wasn't so free anymore.

"Couldn't you come back some other time?" I asked. "I'd like to think about this some." It still hadn't occurred to me that the whole matter was a farce, and that Santa

Claus was actually a Con Clause.

But I signed the agreement and paid $20 down. No sooner had he closed the front door behind himself when I realized I had been victimized by the idea of getting something "free."

The next day I learned not too surprisingly that many of my neighbors had been interviewed for a chance to be the "one" family in our area also. And some of them, like myself, had been chosen, too. But not the smart ones.

I had learned my lesson. No salesman would enter my home again — even if he were selling water and my house were on fire. But it was all in vain.

Since that experience I have been fooled time and again. But not victimized to the point of buying anything. One gentleman entered my home for the purpose of taking a "survey." He turned out to be selling encyclopedias, too.

Another gent wanted to show me a film on "fire safety and prevention." He was selling fire extinguishers.

I've learned my lesson now. I don't let anyone in my house if he's selling anything. The time to stop them is at the door.

Just recently a gentleman knocked at the door. As I opened it he said, "I represent . . ."

"Hold it," I said. "If you're selling anything, I don't want it."

After a few moments of silence and the appearance of shock faded from his face, he explained he was a member of a local church and invited my family to attend services there.

That just goes to prove you can't tell everytime. But there's one thing you can always be sure of: beware of anyone who offers to give you something "free." There's no such thing.

January 1972

NO PANTS FOR THE CHIEF JUSTICE

Citizens shocked by past revelations of human frailty on the lofty U.S. Supreme Court might do well to read a little history.

Otherwise they might conclude from the hubbub raised over court decisions and judges' ethics and incomes that the nation's highest tribunal until recent years has been above criticism.

It hasn't. It has weathered controversies throughout its history, and it will continue to draw fire as long as justices are human.

The nation likes to cloak its judiciary in Olympian legend. The somber robes and retiring manners forced on the bench are all part of the fable of men wiser than men. Yet from the earliest days of American politics, the Supreme Court has bubbled at not infrequent intervals in boiling political stews.

In the early 1800's the Supreme Court was held in such low esteem in some sections of the country that the legendary Chief Justice Marshall was declined tailor service in Raleigh. Writing to his wife, he said he had to hold court without his pants.

In Marshall's time, too, a good-sized segment of the public was ready to impeach the entire Federal bench. During the period, there were six justices in the Supreme Court. In addition to their two annual Washington sessions, they were required to hold circuit court twice a year in their home districts, a condition that brought Justice Marshall frequently to Raleigh.

The history books describe the great jurist as a justice and little more. Personal anecdote recalls him as a man who needed a tailor even more frequently than he patronized one and as an amusing eccentric.

Raleigh was a town of approximately 300 to 500 persons when the Chief Justice paid his semi-annual calls. He usually made the trip from his farm outside of Richmond, Va., in a buggy, accompanied at times by a servant, and stayed at a tavern owned, records say, by a man named Cooke.

Mr. Cooke was not an overly expansive landlord, one account recalls. Raleigh townspeople frequently would meet the head of the Supreme Court out at Cooke's woodpile, hauling in logs.

For all of his judicial eminence, stories have it that Chief Justice John Marshall was not too practical a man.

Once on the trip from Richmond to Raleigh, Marshall and his buggy got hung up on a sapling while taking a short cut through what was then Nathaniel Macon's plantation.

One of Macon's slaves happened to pass, spotted the difficulty and set Marshall free. Reporting the incident to his master, the man was informed he had just helped the Chief Justice of the United States.

"The biggest lawyer in the country," Nathaniel Macon told his hand.

The field hand wasn't impressed.

"Marse Nat," the field hand said, "that may be the biggest lawyer in the United States, but he ain't got sense enough to back a gig off a sapling."

In Richmond, the Chief Justice, whom children's histories paint so impressively, was a frequent butt of poor jokes. A prankster with a turkey approached Mr. Marshall on one occasion and offered him a small coin to carry the bird. It evidentally looked like an easy way to make an honest nickel to the judge. So the Chief Justice of the United States walked down the street behind his temporary employer, lugging a turkey like an errand boy.

One of Marshall's letters written from Raleigh, or to use his spelling, "Rawleigh," on Jan. 2, 1803, offers an insight into the great man's ways.

"My dearest Polly," he wrote:

"You will laugh at my vexation when you hear the various calamities that have befallen me. In the first place, when I came to review my funds, I had the mortification to discover that I had lost 15 silver dollars out of my waistcoat pocket. They had worn through the various mendings the pocket had sustained and had sought their liberty in the sands of Carolina.

"I determined not to vex myself with what could not be remedied and ordered Peter (his servant) take out my clothes that I might dress for court, when to my astonishment and grief, after fumbling several minutes in the portmanteau, staring at vacantly and sweating most profusely, he turned to me with the doleful tidings that I had no pair of breeches."

"You may be sure that this piece of intelligence was not very graciously received; however, after a little scolding I determined to make the best of the situation and immediately set out to get a pair made.

"I thought I should be a sans culotte only one day and that for the residue of the term that I might be well enough dressed for the appearance on the first day to be forgotten. But the greatest of evils, I found, was followed by still greater!

"Not a single taylor in town could be prevailed to work for me. They were all so busy that it was impossible to attend to my wants, however pressing they might be, and I have the extreme mortification to pass the whole time without the important article of dress I have mentioned. I have no alleviation for this misfortune but to hope that I shall be enabled in four or five days to commence my journey homeward and that I shall have the pleasure of seeing you and our dear children in eight or nine days after this reaches you.

"In the meantime I flatter myself that you are well and happy." "J. Marshall."

A newspaper of the time, the Raleigh Register and North Carolina Planter of Jan. 4, 1803, acknowledged the presence of the nation's Supreme Court chief in town with no more notice than:

"On Wednesday the last the Federal Circuit Court for the district commenced its term in this city. Chief Justice Marshall and our District Judge Potter were present. The Grand Jury (of which Walter Alves, Esq., was foreman) being empanelled, the chief justice delivered to them a concise and appropriate charge, fully explaining their duty without the least political intermixture."

Lest somebody jump to the conclusion that young Andrew Johnson was among the tailoring fraternity who refused to supply the judge the needed pants, it should be pointed out that the Raleigh tailor's apprentice who was to become the nation's 17th president wasn't born until 1808.

J. Marshall's toils with the "taylor" were small compared to the storm he was riding out in Washington. The Supreme Court was the center of one of the hottest controversies in our history and Marshall, as head man of the court, was the target of much abuse.

The Federalists in 1801 had managed to shove through legislation which reduced the membership of the bench to five and relieved the justices of their circuit court duties.

The new act divided the country into 16 circuits and created the office of circuit judge for each. With district judges and Supreme Court members, the act gave the nation a total of 38 Federal judges, all — or so the

Republicans claimed — appointed by the Federalists for services received.

The Republicans, as the Democratic Party's members were known then, fought the change from the start. Peeved mainly by the fact that the Federalists had stolen a march in political patronage, the Republican leaders effectively twisted the move into an attack on the Constitution. The Federal court, already too powerful, was being raised to a position higher than the executive and legislative branches, they charged, and, with the increased power, was attempting to twist the Constitution to its own political ends.

Philip R. Thompson, a fiery Virginia Republican, predicted the change was the equivalent of forming a dictatorship of judges.

"Give the Judiciary a check upon the Legislature, allow them the power to declare your laws null and void, and in vain have the people placed you upon the floor to legislate," he warned Congress.

"If they (the judges) have offended against the Constitution, or the laws of the country," he demanded, "why are they not impeached?"

"Our judges are as independent as spaniels," a contemporary newspaper complained.

The battle which finally resolved itself in a victory for the Republicans ended in repeal of the Federalists' 1801 legislation in 1803.

Archibald Henderson, a North Carolina Federalist, whom Marshall termed "unquestionably among the best lawyers of his day," called the Republican program a threat to the nation's democracy.

Another North Carolinian, Robert Williams, described by one account as "an extreme but unskillful Republican," let the facts out by ineptly inquiring on the floor of Congress if a judge could be found guilty of a felony because of his interpretation of the law.

The House rushed the repeal bill through at a midnight session on March 3, 1803, by a vote of 59 to 32. The Senate approved it on April 8. Just to make sure there would be no chance of the Supreme Court declaring the repeal unconstitutional, the Republicans changed the dates of the court sessions from December and June to February and August.

The action, in effect, suspended the Supreme Court for 14 months.

Some of the court's critics would like to suspend it altogether.

1963

CUPS MAKE THE DIFFERENCE

First there is only the click of traffic light mechanisms flashing stop and go at empty intersections, as if they were practicing for the busy day.

The clatter is next — delivery trucks straining and shifting gears, boxes and cans dropping or falling or being slammed through alleys, on sidewalks and in doorways, and doors being rattled, and blinds and awnings being opened or lowered, and all the noises that a city makes awakening joining finally in the chorus a city sings as it goes to work.

Soon all is noise and motion: Heels clattering on pavements, cars carrying the people to their jobs, buses grinding as they stop and start, voices calling. And through it all Raleigh's street sweepers moving with their two-wheel carts.

Al Wilson sweeps every morning on Wilmington Street, and down Hargett and along Davie and in a pattern that carries him, his cart and barrel can and broom on about the same route through the business district in about the same sequence day after day.

He sees the city waking up, and it doesn't excite him. It just happens, he says, and it's not remarkable. He starts his working day, with his cart and barrel and broom 6 o'clock in the morning, he says, with two others, Willie Graham and Mac McNeil.

We start on Fayetteville Street, up at the start of the street, he says as if anybody ought to know that's the way you'd sweep a city. When we get through, he says, we go on other streets. Down Fayetteville Street, down to about where the car lots are. We get all the paper off the streets and we sweep around outside the curbs. We do it to about

198

3, from about 6 to about 3.

Al Wilson has been sweeping that way for about ten years, and he's been working for the city for about 25. Before he came with the city he worked for a grading contractor. He was born in Granville County but he's been in Raleigh ever since he was a boy.

He picks up paper the same way every day, and he empties the litter receptacles here and there the same way and he fills and empties the barrel on his cart two or three times a day, the same way and about the same time and in the same places.

The city and its days, they're routine for Al Wilson and the other two men who, he says, push the other two carts and sweep.

Sometimes people find things in litter receptacles and on streets and sidewalks. They find things and get rewards and become minor celebrities for being honest.

Al Wilson says he never has found anything worth having. Sometimes a penny now and then, but that's all.

But there are things that only he, a sweeper, and Mac and Willie know. They know the new carts with bright plastic barrels and balloon tire bicycle wheels which the city recently bought them are easier than the old carts for aging men to push. And they know why they put paper cups over the hubs of the wheels on the old carts, stuck on like the chrome spinner wheel covers sharp lads put on hotshot cars.

Putting those paper cups on the hubs, Al says with the modesty of a man who has found something not everybody has, putting them on like that, it kept the grease from getting your overalls greasy.

He picked up a cardboard box from the gutter and tore it apart. He put the pieces in his bright new plastic barrel, the same way he had done it yesterday and the day before that and all the yesterdays he's been sweeping. The same way he would tomorrow, with his broom and his barrel and his bright new cart, just as he did with the old cart with the cups on its hubs and just as he would when the new cart begins to drip grease from its axles.

June 1969

A GRATEFUL HEART

A cold wind blows November's
   horn,
Calling through denuded trees,
Calling winter down upon the
   land,
Calling cold rains down, and sleet
Weighs on branches in a dazzling
   glaze,
Bending pines. On mornings window
   glass
Is patterned with traceries in frost.
And yet November has warm days too
As if to point a contrast to the
   cold,
And in November time is set aside
To count our blessings and give
   thanks.
And gathering for Thanksgiving
   Day,
Families find a warmth within
As though November had a soul
Responding to a grateful heart.

LIKE A DAGGER IN OUR HEARTS

Twenty-five years ago on April 12, 1945, in Warm Springs, Ga., a happy young woman ceremoniously poised a knife above a birthday cake.

Eighteen candles burned in pink rosettes on the frosted icing. Beside the cake, atop a telephone switchboard, cold mounds of ice cream waited in saucers.

In a moment the knife would be drawn across the surface of the cake, two happy voices would sing out, "Happy Birthday!" and a Georgia girl working her first assignment as a telephone operator for the "Little White House" would be one year older.

A light flashed on the switchboard... and then another, and another.

The poised knife dropped point foremost among the pink rosettes.

At 4:48 p.m., three wire service representatives were given an announcement.

President Franklin Delano Roosevelt had died at 3:35.

Shortly after 1 p.m. the President was sitting for some sketches. Suddenly his expression tightened.

"I have a terrific headache," he said.

Those were his last words.

By 1:15 p.m. he had lost consciousness.

In a chateau on the Seine a somber-faced colonel quietly announced to a hastily-assembled U. S. Army headquarters staff:

"President Roosevelt is dead. He's dead. That's all I know."

In Paris, Frenchmen cried. Weeks later in Rome an Italian became so emotional that he swept the china and glass from his table in one eloquent gesture of despair.

In Europe, Roosevelt had become a symbol. Would his death cancel all his promises and plans?

Italians, Englishmen, Frenchmen and Germans wondered and waited. . . afraid.

And at Warm Springs, as the funeral train carrying the President's body back to Washington began its journey, a busy Georgia telephone operator aged 18 years and a day glanced momentarily at a birthday cake.

Eighteen puddles of wax lay among the 18 rosettes on its frosted icing.

A knife protruded from its middle like a dagger in a nation's heart.

April 1970

WHAT HAPPENED TO THE SALVE?

Back in the 1920s and 30s, magazines were cluttered with coupon offers and offers of free samples.

Becky was telling how it used to be. Together, we tried to recall some of the old magazines and some of the ads that tantalized us in our childhood.

"Why when I was a child," Becky said, "we used to send in coupons for all sorts of things,"

Remember? Remember sending off for samples of seeds and salves? Remember all the contests there used to be? Remember how you tried to win a pony or a bike — by sending in a coupon telling how many hidden figures you'd seen in the picture?

And in the early days of radio, people used to sit for hours with earphones on their heads listening and taking down the addresses for all the free offers.

And back before anybody had thought of television, people would wait at their mail boxes for the mailman to make his rounds, or congregate at the little community post office. Mail was important then. You'd read every piece. You didn't sort through it the way you do now, throwing the circulars and such away. You read the circulars and opened everything.

And if you were young in those days, you'd watch for the farm magazine the family got and you'd pore over all the ads about contests and free offers. If you'd send in the coupon and would sell the salve, they'd send you a prize. You might even get a B.B. gun for free. The ad on the back cover said you could. You'd look at the ad and the coupon and the picture, and you'd think how wonderful it would be.

Just by sending in a coupon and selling little cans of salve.

No, Becky, people don't send in coupons as they once did. And remembering the salve and how hard it was to sell, we can't blame 'em.

NOTHING SO MUCH AS A CAR

Of all the factors working to shape the future, the automobile is the best known and perhaps least understood. Automobiles have tied the countryside together; they've also created many of its problems. And one thing seems certain: there'll be many more of them, and more of their problems, in the years to come.

Almost nothing else in the past 50 years has had such an effect on the average North Carolinian's life as the automobile. Nothing as much as the automobile has so changed his concepts of distance and time, or so altered his towns and countrysides, or brought town and country so closely together, or so persuasively and curiously convinced him it is so indispensible.

More people today own automobiles than own homes. Many families have two or more automobiles, and it is not considered strange in North Carolina for boys and girls to drive cars on the public highways before they are considered old enough to work for their living and until the voting age was lowered well before they are trusted to vote.

In 1900 there were fewer than 9,000 cars in the entire nation. In 1900 there were few North Carolinians – or other Americans – who had traveled more than 200 miles from home. Today most of us think nothing of making a trip from Raleigh to the coast or the mountains in a day, and many North Carolinians regularly commute hundreds of miles a week between home and work.

One of the earliest automobiles to appear in North Carolina was built at Reidsville by Fletcher Watson Waynick who ran a bicycle shop.

Waynick built three cars around the turn of the century about a year apart.

The first had a one-cylinder five-horsepower engine, a buggy body and buggy wheels. It could go up to 20 miles an hour, and it would run all day at that speed on three gallons of gasoline. Waynick made trips in it from Reidsville to Burlington and Greensboro. His travels in Reidsville were governed by an ordinance specifically adopted to reduce his vehicle as a nuisance and danger to horse-drawn traffic.

He drove to a country church one Sunday. The preacher had to ask him to leave because his "horseless carriage" distracted the congregation so much that the preacher couldn't get the people to come inside to hear the sermon.

The first State requirement for motor vehicle licensing took effect in 1909 under the Office of the Secretary of State. Only 1,681 cars and trucks were registered then, and the owners had to pay a fee of only $5 for a license. After the first year the licenses could be renewed for $1 a year.

The Secretary of State's office continued to act as a motor registration agency until 1925. In 1925 automobile registration and licensing were transferred to the State Revenue Department.

The State Department of Motor Vehicles was established in 1941.

In 1940, there were 669,259 vehicles registered — 516,097 passenger cars and 153,162 commercial vehicles. Included in the commercial vehicle classification were 88,551 trucks and 6,308 buses, and among them were 2,780 common carriers.

Since 1940 the figures haven't merely multiplied; they have exploded.

At the latest official counting, the totals for registration came to 1,711,369 automobiles, 424,634 trucks, 173,618 trailers, 18,471 buses and 18,098 motorcycles.

Once upon a time, boys and girls were lucky if their parents had a car. Now they feel unlucky — and even underprivileged — if they don't have cars of their own. Parking lots have become almost as important at high schools as gymnasiums, and no matter how large the lots may be there are more cars than the lots can hold.

Insurance companies have felt it necessary to raise their rates if there are young drivers in a family. But the higher rates haven't discouraged the youngsters. Parents somehow find — and feel obliged to find — ways to raise the extra dollars so that sons and daughters may drive.

As more and more cars take to the roads, more and more pile up in crashes and collisions — or otherwise fall by the wayside. There are so many wrecks and derelicts that huge automobile salvage yards are growing up and down the roadsides. In them may be seen row upon row of cars of nearly every description and condition. The proprietors of these places can furnish, on short notice, from some car on their lots, almost every part needed for almost any repair.

And if they haven't got the wanted part themselves, they have catalogs and index systems telling in what other lots it may be found.

If you'd tried to explain about automobiles to the average North Carolinian a century ago, he wouldn't have believed you.

And the way we are about automobiles today, it's hardly believable now.

June 1967

SUNDAY'S BELLS

Hear the bells ring
On Sunday morning
In the quiet city
From the steeples
On the square.
Hear them
Ringing, tolling, calling,
Chiming, each a different voice,
In a glad clangor,
Each calling to its people,
Calling in the quiet city
To the churches
On the square.

THE LAST TRAIN TO DALLAS

All his life he had been fascinated by trains. When he was still a small child in Baltimore, he would beg his father to take him to the viaduct from which they could look down on the engines in the big railroad yard. As a growing boy, he would watch trains pass and wave at the engineer and always count the cars.

And on those occasions when his family traveled by train, he would take notice of every feature of the cars in which they rode and remark about every trestle, station and signal light.

He could not afford to ride the trains when he was in school. He hitch-hiked between the university and home, but once he took a train from Richmond to Charlottesville and much later, when he had been married a few years and was on vacation with his wife and two small children in Washington, he took the family on a round trip by train to Baltimore. He was disappointed that neither of the children shared his fascination.

Now he had to go to Dallas, Tex., on business. He had reservations to fly; he always traveled now by air when he had to make long business trips. Otherwise, he drove.

He decided impulsively a few days before he was to leave for Dallas that he would not fly after all. He would go by train — in comfort. He would sleep in a roomette, eat in the dining car and relax in the club car, and he would travel as he always wanted to travel — first class on on train.

He would go by train and recapture all the magic that trains so long had held for him. He would hear again the rhythmic click train wheels make as they roll over the

211

joints in the rails. He would hear the magic noises that travelers hear only in railroad cars — the sound of the diesel horn, the echoes as trains rush past buildings along the tracks, the turbulent sounds trains make as they speed over trestles.

He would hear it all and see it all and feel it all again. And he would carry the memory of it always.

He would go to Dallas on the train because he might never have the time again, or the justification or the chance.

Only a few days ago he had read that many famous trains were headed for retirement. The nation's railroads, the article had said, felt there no longer was sufficient public need for long-distance passenger train service. And the railroads, merging to consolidate their systems and resources, were concentrating on freight service.

So he would go by train to Dallas. And he would write about it so that others of his generation could share the pleasures of his experience. He would tell the story for them so that they could ride with him, as they read, in the Pullman and see in their minds how it was in the dining car and know how it was to sleep in the roomette and picture the countryside sliding by the windows of the club car.

He called the railroad passenger office to make reservations.

He found that he would have to leave Raleigh early Friday evening in order to reach Dallas by rail on Sunday. He could leave the Raleigh-Durham airport at 9 a.m. on Saturday and reach the Dallas airport 30 minutes after noon the same day if he went by plane.

He also found that if he went by train he would not be able to get a sleeper and perhaps no dinner except between Raleigh and Atlanta and certainly not after New Orleans. He would have to sit up all night and travel without meals

212

most of the way. The railroad passenger agent suggested that instead of going by way of Atlanta and New Orleans, he go by way of Richmond and St. Louis. Then he would get a sleeping berth and be sure of eating. But to do that, he'd have to leave Raleigh Friday morning in order to reach Dallas by Sunday morning. And the cost would be approximately twice the cost of the other route.

The dreams he had of all the train trips promised, the memories of how it used to be on the trains and the visions of how it might be on this one last sentimental journey could not endure against the practicalities.

The trip into yesteryear, the Pullman trip to Dallas, would never be taken. And he would never know again perhaps how a diesel horn sounds as you sleep in a Pullman berth and what it is to hear the wheels click over the rails and the train to rush over the trestles. And the story he yearned to write and live would never be written.

May 1968

BLOSSOM BARGAIN

I cannot tell how daffodils
Tell when to show
Their first fingers above the ground.
Nor do I know when they know
The time has come again to raise
Flags of blossoms in the lawn.
But there are those who do
And they come to Raleigh each spring
Before the rest of us know spring has come.
And they bring baskets of daffodils
And their sisters, the jonquils,
To the market and to Capitol Square
For sale, as if to tell city folk
That here is spring at a bargain.

FOR EVERY MAN A BIRD OF HOPE

The broken scarlet body lay like a crumpled red rag against the curb. Only when he looked more closely did he realize it was a bird.

It was a cardinal, he thought, and it probably had flown out of the Square into the path of a car. But do cardinals have yellow tipped tail feathers? He wondered; he never had noticed one with them before.

There are many ways that birds may die. He had heard them on occasions hit the big window at the end of his living room and he had found them dead on the lawn.

There are many ways that a man may die, without dying and without any but those who know him best knowing it. There are many ways a man can be destroyed without shedding his blood.

He can be as dead as the broken bird and still continue in a mockery of life.

He can become so because he withdraws into himself and is as remote to life around him as he would be in a grave. And he can be made so in such subtle ways that none can say for sure how it was done or by whom.

Life is a flame fueled by ego. To live as a man, a man must have a sense of himself and a sense of pride in himself. Crush his vanity, stifle his ambition, scourge his self-respect and no weapon is needed to obliterate the man.

Take away from him all opportunities to make decisions or to pretend he does, ignore him when a word would inspire, criticize when he starves for praise, undermine his confidence and you have destroyed him and only you will know how it was done.

Life is a flame that is easily extinguished and if it is

worth holding to a man must know the poetry of it as well as the pain of it, and there must be a little more room in it for him to keep a little of his vanity, if not a glowing flame at least a spark.

And he must be allowed to hope so that he will not, as the fallen bird, go unnoticed as a scrap in a gutter, unrecognized and vanishing as the world and you race by.

THE MENAGERIE

A sparrow rescued
When fallen from its nest
Now lives in a canary's cage.
A frightened white mouse
Hides in its box on the back porch.
A brown dog whose parents
Were a dachshund and a pekingese
Sleeps on the porch steps.
They are the reminders of a boy
Who in 12 years has filled a house
With reminders, hopes and wants.
And now, in his absence on a holiday,
I survey his menagerie and his cluttered room
And sort parts of broken radios
From an arsenal of toy guns
And find among the countless things
A boy of 12 keeps in disarray
The pattern that will become a man's.
And I wonder when the pattern is filled
If he still will have room in it
For the rescue of a sparrow
And the care of a frightened mouse
And the love of a mongrel dog.
And if he does, then his life, and mine,
Will be the richer for compassion.

EVERYBODY NOW BY THE NUMBERS

Nothing about the letter was startling. It was merely another bit of evidence of the fitting of people to bureaucracy's forms.

It was a form to be filled out so that two young people could be numerically indexed.

One of them was 12 and the other 16. Their father, as trustee of two small savings accounts he had established in their names, was to provide the information the form requested so that the 12-year-old and the 16-year-old could be issued Internal Revenue numbers until they could get Social Security numbers.

And why not? Everybody and everything these days has a number and sometimes several.

There's a telephone number. No longer is it Raleigh 2-2055. It is or was TEmple 2-2055 and even that tissue of identity has given way to a number. TEmple has become 83. You can dial clear across the continent without hearing a human voice until you get your party, all by numbers.

There's your auto license tag. If you have one you also have an automobile registration number, model number, engine number and driver's license number, and, if you live in town, a city tag number.

Add to these a house number, box number, route number, credit card number, draft registration number, insurance policy numbers, Veterans Administration claim number, subscription renewal numbers and not the least, that Social Security number. You don't have one? There's a provision to cover that. A housewife without one gets one, or an identifying number in lieu of one, to use in reporting income taxes, even if she has no income.

Add it up and it comes to the point that in the world of business machine card sorters and electronic indexers and the like, you are not a person anymore but a composite of codes.

And the time may come someday, as electronic indexing and by-the-numbers processing becomes the fact rather than the prospect, when names may remain only among friends.

You'll not be John Smith. You'll be 832-2055.

Where it all will lead nobody can say for certain.

In the newspaper business, it leads inevitably to "30." In the crass old days before reporters became journalists, "30" was the way stories ended.

And that's the number now for this.

July 1968

THE FAMILY DOCTOR

The glory today is in big medicine — big research, big hospitals and big city practice. But there still are doctors who choose to practice where good practitioners are needed most, in the rural areas and small towns. Some of them are practicing here in North Carolina. Here, cloaked in the anonymity which the ethics of their profession wraps around its members, several of them comment on their problems and their satisfactions.

Dr. G. was in the prime of manhood, sturdy and self-assured in one of those white nylon blouses some doctors wear when they work.

His office was a one-story block structure with the lines of a ranch house; he shared it on the outskirts of town with a dentist. He had finished with one patient, a child, and he was prescribing for a woman. His nurse came in to report that the mother of a small boy he had treated wanted to know if the youngster would be able to return to school the next week. The telephone rang bringing a question from some woman patient wondering if she should continue her pills.

People kept coming or calling, and he still had calls waiting to be answered when his nurse and receptionist began closing the office for the weekend.

Approximately 1,200 general practitioners like Dr. G. have offices across North Carolina. About 800 of them are members of the North Carolina Academy of Family Practice. Several are located in and around Raleigh, and a number of specialists in internal medicine, pediatrics and the other fields including even obstetrics and surgery often serve as general practitioners for some of their patients.

Rural areas and small towns losing their older doctors are having difficulties attracting younger physicians. The increasing national demands for medical services is one reason. The local lack of facilities often is another. But mainly people have become accustomed to going to larger towns and to medical centers and in too many instances community groups expressing the greatest need for medical services really want 'first aid' and 'emergency' treatment for their convenience. A doctor can't survive on this type of medicine. Nor can one doctor make it alone. If there is to be one physician in a community, there ought to be two, so that one may spell the other occasionally and so that both may have time occasionally for relief from the incessant pressures to which all good doctors are heir.

There is a shortage of doctors but the medical profession says the shortage is largely one of general practitioners in rural areas and small towns. There are surgeons and other specialists looking for places to begin practice, medical spokesmen say, while places for family doctors go unfilled.

Some communities in North Carolina have attempted to attract physicians by forming community corporations to build offices, clinics and even homes for them. Some have guaranteed a certain volume of practice, and the doctor hunt in some communities makes nearly as many promises and offers as the industry-hunting campaigns.

Dr. G. thought some of the attempts and some of the doctors involved in them were headed for failure.

"Putting up a clinic at every crossroads that wants one, and putting a general practitioner in it won't solve the doctor shortage," Dr. G. said. "I know; I went through it.

"They put up a clinic, a little seven-bed hospital, and I took it over and bought it," he said, "and I went broke. It took me five years to get on my feet again."

221

There's more to the problem than that, he said; the people in the area not only have got to want a doctor, they've got to be willing to patronize him. That's the heart of the problem, he said. Many of the places that bring doctors in think everything is done when they've finished their campaign and built the office and clinic.

When the doctor takes over, he said, that's the end of it. The people in the area see him when it's not convenient for them to go to the doctors in town or they use him only for emergencies.

He's there like the crossroads store, for the things they forgot in town or don't consider important enough to go to town to see about. A doctor, Dr. G. said, won't last long in a situation like that.

* * *

Dr. McC. is a young bachelor and his office is in a shopping center on the eastern side of the city. Mothers in the suburban area bring their children to see him when it's not handy to go to their regular pediatricians, and people use him for the things that don't seem to warrant going into the city for visits to their regular doctors.

His practice was growing, but slowly. He's gone now. He went to Chapel Hill for postgraduate studies and stayed to become part of the University's medical complex.

* * *

Dr. Don M. is a family man who, although only just past 40, has become a leading figure in the affairs of his rural county. He's a general practitioner who performs surgery, delivers babies and can serve nearly every medical need his patients present.

He took over his practice from the estate of an older

doctor who had died. He has a clinic equipped to do many of the things small hospitals do, including X-rays; Dr. M. knows that specialty, too.

Once a week he and his wife leave town, traveling to Raleigh for a respite from the relentless demands of rural-smalltown medicine. Another doctor takes his calls then, but on the other days — and night — Dr. M. knows whether there's company for supper or whether he is counting on catching up on his sleep, there'll be interruptions.

* * *

"A general practice in a small town or out in the country is hard medicine," Dr. S. said. Dr. S. was nearing the age when men in other lines look towards retirement. That wasn't likely in his case, he said, but if he could find a younger man he could work with and who could take over some of the load, he wanted to split his practice. The trouble, though, he said, is that there's not much to interest a young man, and they're hard to come by.

"A general practice in a place like this," he said, "means you're at the office, or answering calls, seeing patients all the time. Out in the country like this a lot of the people work in town or in the mills here and there. They need you when they get home. It should be the end of the day for you, but it's often the busiest.

"In the morning you see office patients, sew up cuts, take care of a broken arm for a boy hurt at school, run out to see a woman who is expecting, and see about patients you referred to the hospital. The afternoon is more of the same, and then the evening routine begins."

* * *

223

In a small community, Dr. G. said, you're a target for every drive and solicitation. Everybody thinks the doctor is getting rich; everybody wants something from him. If you'd specialized, he said, you could limit your practice, ration your hours and make as much or more with less strain on yourself.

"But I'm glad I'm in general practice," he said. "I wouldn't have it any other way."

A general practice, he said, is medicine in the fullest sense of service and satisfaction. It's not easy to impress that on others, not even others in the profession.

"A rural or small town practice as a life's work is a challenge, he said, and it carries with it the satisfaction that comes from doing what you know must be done.

"But you can't stay at it; not unless the people share your conviction that the rural and small town general practitioner is important. Even that won't help unless they can convince themselves that you're there for more than just emergencies and the sickness that to them don't seem important enough to be treated at the nearest city or big town."

"I know how it is," the doctor said. "I've been through it. And I'm still as sure as when I started that the physician's greatest satisfaction is in serving the patient and that the general practitioner best fills that need."

April 1971

THE OLD SOLDIERS

On V-E Day, student protestors marched in the city and demonstrated on the campuses, and the fact that May 8 was the 25th anniversary of the end of the war in Europe went unnoticed in the anger and dissent.

Back in the forties the mood was different. Many of the editors and reporters who worked to put the stormy news of May 8, 1970, into print were so fired with patriotism back then they didn't wait to be drafted. Like many other North Carolinians of their generation, they enlisted or wangled commissions and left old reliables like Tony McKevlin and Neil Hestor to put out the paper with a staff of the overaged males, girl replacements and 4-Fs. One of the girl replacements, Marjorie Hunter, was to prove a better newspaperman than the boys she replaced. She's in Washington now as a top hand for The New York Times.

I was one of the 4-Fs, but I was not then on the paper. I had just arrived in Raleigh to work for United Press, a job I landed mainly because I supposedly was draft-exempt.

Somehow I managed, after being turned down twice, to get a waiver of my status and entered the Fort Bragg induction station with Woodrow Price, who then was a staffer for the Raleigh AP bureau.

Woody made something of a mark his first day by scoring highest for that week's crop of inductees on the Army's intelligence test. His score was so high I was sure they'd make him a colonel or better. I took consolation that I had not let UP down completely; I scored higher than he on the mechanical aptitude test, which is remarkable when you consider I still can't use more than two fingers to type.

In neither case did our scores matter. Woodrow wound up in the Pacific as a radar technician and I in Europe as a military correspondent. Woody achieved fame as the man who cleaned up Tinian, becoming the first of the environmentalists by scouring the beaches for pop bottles discarded by GIs and turning them in for the deposit. I became known as the only reporter foolish enough to cover operations wiser full-fledged civilian war correspondents either ignored or considered too tedious to cover for themselves.

Charles Craven, now a featured columnist, also served in Europe. Under circumstances I still don't fully understand, he got a hero's medal, the Purple Heart. All Charlie has ever explained is that he fell down a railroad cut.

Jim Whitfield, now a business editor, made master sergeant. Bill Humphries, now a quiet-spoken farm editor, survived OCS and became a first lieutenant.

Bill Womble, now retired after years as a city editor, was a Coast Guard petty officer. Bob Brooks, a news editor, came out of the Marines as a captain. Bob Lynch, whose byline appears regularly over all sorts of stories, was wounded in action as a Marine in the Pacific.

Herb O'Keef, city editor when Woody and I started our careers on the paper in 1946, saw service in the Pacific Theater as an Army Intelligence non-com. Now he's the completely demilitarized editor of the city's afternoon daily.

Sam Ragan came out of World War II neither boasting nor griping. Rising from state editor to managing editor and finally to executive editor, he made us, along with such notable alumni as Simons Fentress, Neil Morgan and Jay Jenkins, one of the best and most productive teams of reporters in the country. Appropriately he's now the editor and publisher of his own newspaper.

I don't suppose any of us, in all the time we spent together on the paper or in the many bull sessions we had before we drifted apart, ever really exchanged our World War II experiences. Very few of the old soldiers of that war — the businessmen, farmers, workers, professional men and plain citizens of 1970 — have. And few of us came home feeling we'd been heroes or had done anything more than millions of other GIs had done to make victory possible.

We've never gathered together to celebrate V-E Day, or V-J Day or anything else related to our war.

And now, 25 years after peace was restored in Europe and the World Made Safe for Democracy, the world is so sick of war that our war, and our part in it, no longer matters.

A BOY AGAIN

If I could be a boy again
Would I still do all the things I did?
Would I still make all my old mistakes?
Would I still want to know the whys and hows
Of the many questions I once asked
And wonder why things had to be?
And puzzle over as many mysteries,
And wish the same things could come true
And still find magic in the world?
No, there is nothing I would change,
Neither sorrows nor delights.
And I would be a better man
If I could be a boy again.

DECEMBER'S STAR

Briskly now on bright December
    days,
So precious in December's cold
    regime,
When winter's cachet seals the
    closing year,
Shoppers scurry through the
    towns,
And children wait impatiently,
    counting,
Asking when will Christmas come,
    and
Among the stars that light
    December skies,
A star among the many shines
    for Him
As it shone there when the
wisemen came
And shepherds tending flocks first
    knew
The Message and rejoiced the
    Birth
That now of our December makes
Both a celebration and a prayer.

A HULLABALOO FOR CHRISTMAS

Twenty years ago or so I wrote a bitter article decrying the commercialization of Christmas.

The way the stores started the Christmas season well before Thanksgiving struck me as a desecration of the holy feast. I took angry exception to the playing of Christmas music from loudspeakers to get shoppers in the mood for Christmas buying, and I charged the jingle bells of Christmas had been rung out by the jingle of the cash register.

Well, Christmas still comes early in the stores. The decorations go up on our main streets just as they did then, before Thanksgiving, and the cash registers still jingle, and the commercialization is even more intense.

I suppose I could still make the same charges and use the same angry words, but my mood has mellowed.

In fact, I find now that I can't wait for Christmas. The merriment can't start too soon for me any more. I'm glad when they start stringing the lights and hanging the artificial wreaths in the business district, and I like the Christmas music echoing through November's streets.

I'm not condoning desecrations; it's just that I'm finding as I grow older that there is more to Christmas than buying gifts and hoping you'll get the equal or better in return. I'm learning that the hullabaloo of Christmas sales and Christmas parades and the hard-sell Santa Claus really don't matter if you can hear the hymn above the din.

And so I commend you, let the Christmas lights go on even earlier than now. Let the merchants drown the shoppers in Christmas' glad tidings. Let the cash registers ring and the shopping center Santas come as early as they will.

231

Because if you have Christmas in your heart, the spirit of it will carry you through the cacophony. And if you have a place to be on Christmas Day with those who love Christmas too, and if you will hear in your church the Christmas story told again, you will know in your heart when Christmas comes that it is a miracle never tarnished. And you will wish its spirit could prevail not only from before Thanksgiving but through every month of your years.

A CHRISTMAS TO REMEMBER

The boy stood alone in the darkness at the head of the stairs. In the dim light of a Christmas dawn, he saw a man at the foot of the staircase. The boy thought it was Santa Claus, and he was afraid. The rest of the family — the boy's father and mother and his sister Frances — were still in bed. The boy was three and a half. He was anxious to go downstaris and see his presents, but he dared not try to slip past the man.

Snow lay on Baltimore's streets and on the white steps of the houses. As the boy waited, watching the man, he could hear the muffled sounds of an occasional car or milk wagon as the sleeping city began to stir.

The boy tried to make out the man. If it was Santa Claus, why was he still in the house and why didn't he move? And if it was Santa Claus, why did his clothes look so dark and why didn't his white beard show?

The more the boy thought about the man, the more he wished the man would go away.

Silently, cautiously, the boy moved away from the stairs. He tiptoed back to his bedroom and crawled into his bed.

When the boy awoke again, the sun was up, his parents were up. He could hear their voices downstairs. It was safe now.

The boy hurried down the stairs. As he took the last step down to the front hall he saw somebody had left a coat draped over the newel post.

Was that what had looked like a man in the half light? Or had he really seen a man?

The boy was three and a half, and he had no time on a

Christmas morning to ponder such questions. It was enough that Christmas had come and that in the parlor with the sliding doors at the foot of the stairs in the row house on a street of white stoops in Baltimore he was witnessing and living the first Christmas he would remember.

The Christmas Scavengers

The tight little grey house on Cinder Road was hardly big enough to hold Christmas and so many children. There had been rumors in school that Santa Claus was just make-believe, but the boy refused to believe them. He had a theory: if you stopped believing in Santa Claus, you'd stop getting presents.

Since his family had moved into the little house, the boy had made friends with the children of a junkman who lived in a shack beside the railroad, a pasture and two stone walls away.

The junkman's boys seldom washed or worked and did all the things the boy's parents told him were dangerous, yet never got hurt. They were great scavengers and they were always bringing things home from the dump of a nearby State children's hospital.

Whenever the boy could slip away, he would go with them to the dump and dig out of the rubbish abandoned toys, games and books and, occasionally and best of all, cars of discarded electric trains.

The boy never fully understood why so many exciting and valuable things were thrown on the dump. And he would smuggle home not only toy dump trucks and tractors but Tom Swift books and other books that caught his fancy.

When the boy's father came home from the city where he worked to be with his family on Christmas, the boy proudly displayed a few volumes from his dump heap library. His father asked him sharply if he didn't know the children at the hospital had infectious diseases and that the books probably were filled with germs.

Well, the boy rationalized, the Bloom boys go to the dump all the time and they never get sick.

The boy's father took the books and put them in the oven and turned on the stove to bake out the germs. It might have worked, but in the excitement of Christmas, the books were forgotten until somebody smelled something burning.

A dozen Tom Swift adventures were baked to a crisp, germs and all.

If it hadn't been Christmas, and if the boy hadn't already read the stories, it would have been tragic because the boy had planned to trade those Tom Swifts for a picture history of the Spanish American war and a Lionel engine — also from the dump.

No Goats for Christmas

The year the boy got the goat wagon for Christmas most children were lucky if they got anything. The country was deep in the Depression and families considered themselves blessed if they could afford something special for Christmas dinner.

The goat wagon was built exactly like a full-size farm wagon with steel-rimmed wooden wheels that were smaller in front than in the rear, a removable wagon seat and a body with detachable sideboards and a tail gate. It looked like it was meant for work. Its hubs stuck out and scraped things when the boy tried to play with it in the house. His mother told him he would have to take it outside and use it to bring in the wood.

The boy thought since it was a goat wagon he ought to have a goat to pull it, but remembering his last experience with goats he knew that was not to be. One day when his father had an Essex touring car with a blue celluloid sun visor over the windshield, they had driven to visit their Aunt Emma. It turned out to be an expensive afternoon.

Aunt Emma's boys raised goats. A billy goat climbed up on the Essex and punched its sharp hooves through the fabric roof and chewed up the sun visor.

So the boy used the goat wagon to bring in the wood, pulling it himself, knowing he'd never have a goat to harness and wishing that next Christmas he could get a bicycle.

Christmas Is in the Heart

The boy was grown now. In not many years more his daughter and son would have homes and families of their own. On Christmas morning drinking coffee and reading, he thought of all the Christmases he had known and how each, in good years and bad, always was special.

His children had long passed the age when a few toys would make the day. Most of their presents this Christmas were clothes and as he sat and waited for the house to awaken he mused sadly that Christmas had lost its magic for them. On Christmases past they would already have been down to see what Santa had brought and they would be in the living room by the tree chattering and laughing and tearing open packages.

He lit his pipe and tried to concentrate on his mystery novel, but his thoughts kept wandering.

He heard paper being ripped in the living room. Somebody had finally come downstairs. Somebody finally had decided you couldn't be indifferent on Christmas. And he heard his daughter speak to his son.

She spoke softly so as not to awaken mother, and the boy whispered an excited reply. There was a yelp of delight and a suppressed squeal and then laughter. And his daughter called out to him:

"Daddy," she said, "come in and see the presents. You ought to see what we've got. It's the best Christmas ever."

He laid aside his book and his years fell away and he was a boy again. He went into the living room and when he saw the children on the floor, their faces bright with Christmas wonderment, he remembered all his Christmases past and he knew then that none of them was as wonderful as the Christmas that awaited him now.

HOW TO MAKE YOUR CHRISTMAS MERRIER

Very few of us can be the Magi at Christmastime.

But by giving of ourselves we can give a greater gift.

Very few of us can hope again to know at Christmastime the magic that Christmas holds for children.

But all of us can in some small way make some child happier.

All of us can search our hearts and extend ourselves to make this a better Christmas for all of those whose lives touch ours.

All of us can bury old resentments and turn away wrath and wipe away in the days that remain until Christmas Eve the tears we have brought to another's eyes.

All of us can forgive . . . and ask forgiveness.

All of us can reply to anger with understanding, and respond to bitterness with compassion that even the most bitter cannot withstand as Christmas comes.

And we can look for the Star rather than the tinsel.

And for the Miracle in the Manger rather than the measure of whether we get from life as much as we give.

And if only a few of us will do these things, if only you and I will forget ourselves and think of Him, then Christmas will be merrier for all who know us.

And we will know again the merriment at Christmas we knew as children.

And we will know again the faith of a child.

And our faith will enrich us more than all the Magi's riches.

For we will know Christmas as it is meant to be.

THE GIFT OF LIFE

The greatest gift you can give is not money but a donation you can make at no expense to yourself which will help save lives, relieve suffering and advance medical research.

A woman gave a kidney a while ago to save a stranger's life, and the story of her sacrifice made news across the nation.

People in North Carolina not only give kidneys and other organs but their entire bodies to North Carolina medical centers to help save other peoples' lives or advance medical research, and nobody outside their immediate families and the doctors involved ever hear of it.

You can make such a donation, knowing unless you want the word spread, your secret will be kept.

It's easily done. Several dozen bodies a year are received this way by the Duke University Medical Center in Durham. Others are given the same way to the University of North Carolina Medical Center at Chapel Hill and the Bowman Gray (Wake Forest University) Medical Center at Winston-Salem.

It's easily done, but you have to do it yourself, and you should be sure your next of kin knows of your plans.

You should be able to get information on how to make the arrangements from your doctor. Or you may write to the Duke Medical Center, Durham; the University of North Carolina Medical School, Chapel Hill; the Bowman Gray School of Medicine, Winston-Salem, or the School of Allied Health and Social Professions at East Carolina University, Greenville.

The gift may be made through a provision in your will or filling out a Uniform Donor Card. You can get the card from any of the medical schools. To get one from Duke, write to the Department of Anatomy, Box 3011, Durham, N.C. 27706.

The Uniform Donor Card is being adopted throughout the nation and is designed to be carried in your wallet or purse.

The card enables a donor to execute a legal gift to the medical center of his choice, to show whether he wants to donate all of his body, or any needed organs or parts, or only specified organs or parts, or to define any limitations or special wishes. It must be signed by the donor and two witnesses.

Since you will want the medical center to get the body promptly after death, particularly if organs and parts are to be used for transplants, you should inform your family, minister, lawyer and doctor that you have such a card. Otherwise, there may be delays in notifying the medical center. Days and sometimes weeks often elapse before a will is read, or personal effects examined.

Not many of us can leave large bequests to charities or make big contributions to good causes, but any of us can match a millionaire's largess by helping medical science save lives and carry forward research.

There is a continuing and growing need for human bodies and organs for medical education, research, transplantation and other forms of treatment.

Recent advances in medical science have greatly improved the prospects of saving lives and restoring health by transplantation. Today, many persons can be helped by the transplantation of organs or tissues, many of which can be used after the death of the donor.

Nearly all religious groups in the United States approve

such bequests. Clergymen of most denominations are willing to assist and advise families and to arrange appropriate memorial services.

"An increasing number of persons are willing their bodies for medical research," a Duke Medical Center spokesman said. "These people are from all walks of life and are making their donations not only to Duke but to all other medical schools as well."

In some cases you can specify that certain vital parts, such as the eyes, are to be donated for special uses.

For about 25 years, corneal transplantation has been an established means of restoring vision in blindness due to disease of the cornea. Transplantation of the kidneys, skin tissue, bone tissue, and other organs and tissues is performed frequently to help patients return to health.

Procedures for the transplantation of the heart, the lungs, the liver and the pancreas are now in the early stages of development and some remarkable successes have been achieved.

The need for tissues and organs for transplantation and other medical uses far exceeds the available supply. Patients who need transplants of the cornea usually have to wait weeks or months before a donated eye is available.

Patients with extensive, deep burns of the skin need their bodies covered temporarily by skin grafts from a donor to allow time for gradual, permanent coverage by grafts of their own skin.

Transplants of human bone tissue are frequently needed in the surgical treatment of complicated fractures and other disorders of the bones and joints. There is a continuous shortage of human pituitary glands. The temporal bone of the skull is needed for research to improve the treatment of deafness.

Through the North Carolina Eye and Human Tissue

241

Bank, the Eye Association of America and the International Eye Bank Association, eyes to be transplanted may be readily shipped to distant points if not urgently needed in North Carolina.

In a kidney-sharing program initiated in 1969, a number of hospitals in Maryland, the District of Columbia, Virginia, North Carolina, Georgia and Tennessee are cooperating to make the best use of kidneys which become available and to get each kidney to a patient with a good tissue match for successful transplant.

Pituitary glands are delivered to the National Pituitary Agency, which extracts the hormone and distributes it to doctors for the treatment of patients who need it.

Your family doctor, eye specialist or kidney specialist or endocrinologist may be able to help you get the addresses of these agencies. Or you can write to: Transplantation Program, Box 3052, Duke University Medical Center, Durham, N.C. 27706.

Most medical schools will pay to have the body delivered to them, within certain geographical limitations. The Duke Medical Center, for example, will pay for any necessary embalming and for the transportation of a body within North Carolina for a distance of 200 miles or less, at fixed rates known to most funeral directors in the state.

If the donor wishes to leave instructions that his estate bear the cost of removing the body, the limited funds of the medical schools can be preserved for further education and research.

Once the body reaches its destination it can be used for teaching, research, or transplants, or for all three purposes.

You can give but you can't sell. Those stories you may have read or heard about people who have sold their bodies are in these times only myths.

No medical school can pay an individual before his

death a sum that will assure the delivery to a medical school. It may have been done in the dark days of grave robbers, but it is not done now, and hasn't been done for a least the last half century.

You hear, too, that the unclaimed bodies of paupers and executed criminals are a main source of cadavers for medical students. In accordance with the anatomical laws of North Carolina, an unclaimed body must be turned over to the Anatomical Board, but the supply of these isn't nearly enough to supply medical school needs.

Medical schools depend on bodies to help teach aspiring doctors how living bodies function. There are other ways, but in subjects such as anatomy, bodies are basic to the course.

The reasons people give their bodies are perhaps as numerous as the bodies that are donated. Some do it to spare their families the expenses of funerals. Some do it because they think what is left when they are gone should be used to help others live longer.

As the late Dr. J. E. Markee of Duke put it once: "A great many people are motivated by the fact that 'the dead can teach the living.' Some people feel they have received a great deal that was of benefit to them from medical centers and, consequently, take this way of trying to pay a moral obligation to the center. Some have had rare diseases and feel that the contribution of their bodies for instruction may contribute to the treatment of these rare diseases."

There are many reasons and the way is simple. You can do it. But you have to arrange to do it before you die.

WE'D TRADE BEARS WITH DANIEL BOONE

Hold your head high, friend. The suggestions that you and the rest of us 20th Century Americans lack the grit and gumption of our pioneer forebears aren't true. They are refuted daily by the realities of our do-it-yourself age.

The Indians and hardships our ancestors faced can't compare with the involvements we face when we buy.

Like assembling the things that are sold today unassembled.

Like putting together a lawn and garden storage house kit.

Sure, the pioneers built cabins out of logs and hand-hewed timbers for their houses. But they didn't have to match Upright 720 to Crosspiece 609 or, reading from a folio of "E-Z Step Instructions," Line up 30 screw holes and insert in sequence 30 screws.

Dan'l Boone might have killed all those bears he's credited with, but could he have discovered in time to avoid putting the roof panels on backwards that the arrows on the instruction sheet somehow pointed in the opposite directions from the arrows on the panels?

And all the little black plastic doodads that fit between the two pairs of black metal uprights so as to look like wrought iron scroll-work. Could any of the Indian fighters in our folklore have fitted a screwdriver through each filigree doohickey and set the screws without breaking off at least one curlicue?

How about it, Davy Crockett? How about it, Mr. Lewis and Clark? Did you ever come up against anything like that in the wilderness and on your expeditions?

How about things like sliding doors? Could any

244

frontiersmen you've ever heard about have put the little nylon rollers on at just the exact angle so that the doors would glide on — and not stick in — their tracks?

Hardly. Hardly at all.

Because we've been hardened to it. We're conditioned. We've been through assembling ordeals that would have turned Mr. Boone's hair grey and curled the tail on Mr. Crockett's coonskin cap.

We've been through Christmas. We've wrestled with the kits of cardboard dollhouses and put together cardboard electric ranges (with make-believe burners, powered by flashlight batteries, that light up when the child turns the knob) and cardboard kitchen sinks and refrigerators that defy the handiest handyman if he so much as misreads or skips an item on the instruction form. And we've dealt with bicycles that come in cartons and all the other toys that come broken down and have to be put together stealthfully at midnight on Christmas Eve.

Indians and bears, and stampeding buffalo, sure they were problems.

They were problems you could settle with your trusty musket or flintlock and a steady aim. You didn't have to tackle them single-handed with a screwdriver and a folded square yard of E-Z instructions that never quite set out all the instructions you discover you need.

GRANDFATHER'S FAVORITE CHRISTMAS DAY

Christmas has always been a family day at Granddaddy's. It always will be as long as Granddaddy and Nannie live. It will always be a day, even as the grandchildren grow older, when every member of the family learns anew the richer meanings of the Christmas tradition.

The seven grandchildren all are school age now. Betsy, Nancy, Mary Jane and Catherine have outgrown dolls, In a few more Christmases, Bert, Martha and Jimmy will have outgrown toys. None of them ever will outgrow Granddaddy's love. Nor will they or any of the family soon forget how it is to be with him on Christmas.

On Christmas Day the big white house with the bungalow roof and dormers, where Granddaddy and Nannie live in the quiet little rural community, is Christmas all over. Christmas dinner cooks in the kitchen. The big dining room has a Christmas air. And the front bedroom where hardly anybody goes except on Christmas and where only rarely now anybody sleeps, is waiting, with a Christmas tree and stacks of gaily wrapped packages.

The parlor as usual is reserved for visitors; even on Christmas it's a room apart. When the packages have been opened the children will go with their presents to the rooms the family normally uses, to the bedroom where Granddaddy and Nannie sleep and to the narrow "conservatory" ajoining it with its furniture with floral cushions and its windowsills lined with pots of African violets. And the older girls will steal away to the back bedroom where their mothers used to sleep and where

Mary Jane and Catherine now and then hide to share their teenage confidences.

The Christmas excitement begins when the three daughters and their husbands and the seven grandchildren arrive in mid-morning. Mary Jo, the nearest of the daughters, lives only a few miles south in a nearby town. Lucille Plummer, the youngest and the mother of four of the grandchildren, lives roughly 30 miles southeast. Janie and her husband and their two have a home in Raleigh.

Granddaddy and Harry, Granddaddy's man-of-all-jobs, are waiting for them — Harry at the garage in the backyard where he has a room and Granddaddy in the kitchen or in the yard with Harry — to help them carry in the gifts they will add to those already in the front bedroom around the Christmas tree.

When the children were younger and before Sweet Mama died, the three cars would stop at Sweet Mama's house before driving up the street to Granddaddy's.

Sweet Mama was the children's great grandmother and the mother of Nannie and Nannie's two sisters, Mama 'Cile and Agnes, the children's great aunts who are the other regular members of all family gatherings.

But always the real Christmas was with Granddaddy and Nannie, with Sweet Mama when she was living sitting in the center of things and enjoying the excitement even more than the children.

The seven children already have had a taste of Christmas in their homes. They have seen what Santa Claus has brought. They have picked out their favorite presents and they have brought along things to show to one another and to their grandparents.

Now, finally at Granddaddy's house, they are ready for Christmas in earnest.

Now, after the cars have been unloaded and everybody

has welcomed everybody else, they are in the front bedroom with their grandparents and parents and their great aunts waiting eagerly for the first of the wrapped Christmas gifts to be distributed.

Granddaddy has arranged the boxes in piles for each of them. He calls their names, with the youngest first, and in moments the room is alive with a merry confusion.

Soon gift wrappings are scattered everywhere. Now the room seems filled with children and with squeals and laughter and exclamations of delight and excitement. There are presents for Nannie and Granddaddy and for Mama Cile and Agnes and for each of the daughters and the three sons-in-law. There are presents for Harry. There are toys for Bert and Martha and Jimmy and the things teenage girls want for Betsy, Nancy, Mary Jane and Catherine.

There is something for everybody and more than enough for all.

Granddaddy and Nannie have taken care to give to each and all in equal measure. If one grandson gets a catcher's mitt, both get catcher's mitts. If one granddaughter gets a new dress, all get new dresses.

If one grandchild gets a hug and a kiss, all get hugged and kissed in turn as do their mothers. They are all, no matter how old they have grown and no matter how grown up they may feel, still Granddaddy's babies. And on Christmas Day his pleasure in all of them is as unlimited as his generosity.

The gifts now all are opened. The daughters and Nannie and Great Aunts Mama Cile and Agnes are talking. The toys are being tested and some already are needing repair. Granddaddy is sorting out the debris and he and Harry and the sons-in-law are clearing away the empty boxes and putting aside such things as now may be packed into their cars.

The time has come to eat. Nannie and the daughters now are in the kitchen. Each of the daughters has brought something for the Christmas meal and Nannie as always has cooked and fixed enough to feed twice as many as will come to the table.

There is country ham. There's a turkey succulent and savory. There are heaping servings of butter beans, snap beans, stewed squash with onions, corn pudding, scalloped oysters and scalloped tomatoes, oyster dressing and Nannie's own variety of bread crumb dressing.

There are pickled peaches and watermelon rind preserves and fruit salads and congealed salads and pound cakes, plain cakes, spice cakes, upside down cakes, fruit cakes, blackberry pudding, gelatin with whipped cream and sweet potato pie. Nannie is responsible for most of it but each daughter has contributed a share.

Gradually the children are rounded up. The family collects to eat, the grown-ups in the dining room and the children in the breakfast room and at a folding table in the kitchen.

Now they all are at their places and Nannie tells Granddaddy it's time for the blessing. And they join in giving thanks for all they have and share together.

Two houses down the street there's a little wooden church with a wooden steeple where the family goes together on Sundays when there are services. The daughters and the grandchildren always come to Granddaddy's on "church Sundays" and many other Sundays, too. There, in the little church, the children have heard over the years the story of the Christ Child and the First Christmas and they are reminded of it now as they bow their heads and the blessing is said.

As the prayer is finished, Granddaddy is moved to say the names of each of them, the daughters and the

249

sons-in-laws and the seven children.

There never, he says, has been as nice a Christmas with everybody able to be together and all of them enjoying it so and with so much to be thankful for.

And the children laugh because that is what Granddaddy said last Christmas and the Christmas before that and all the Christmases past they can remember.

And that, they know, he would say if there were nothing, if there were only the group of them gathered there sharing the Christmas spirit. That he would say if there were no toys, nor turkey and ham, nor cakes, nor presents.

The family. . . his children seated with him and their children sharing their joy with him, that is Christmas as it is meant to be and ought to be. And that, for families like Granddaddy's in the old houses in the old communities everywhere in North Carolina this Christmas, will be Christmas as it is.

THE CHRISTMAS CLOSET

The little house stood on a rise overlooking a ravine with a large maple tree in its front yard and a gaunt, thorny locust tree in back.

It had a small porch with a shed roof below its front gable sheltering its front door, an "A" roof with weather-stained cedar shingles and a chimney in the middle, mullioned sash windows and weather-boarding that needed paint.

It was a crowded little house and now with the approach of Christmas it was a house overcrowded with children's hopes.

It was not a house for secrets or for hiding things. The children had ready access to its only two closets. One was at the head of the stairs. The other was under the stairs. Neither had a lock on its door.

There were only four rooms — two downstairs and two up under the roof. One of the downstairs rooms was used as a kitchen and for family meals, washing, ironing and Saturday night baths. The other was furnished with a large round oak table with a pedestal base and matching chairs, an oak sideboard, a treadle sewing machine, a large imitation leather rocker and an imitation leather davenport that opened into a bed.

The kitchen was at the front of the house. It had a large black kitchen range with wood stacked beside it and a kitchen cabinet with shelves for dishes and a bin for flour at the top, drawers for knives, forks and spoons and cupboards at the bottom for pots and pans. An ice box of varnished oak with a well in the top for a block of ice stood against one wall. A wash basin and a water bucket with a dipper in it sat on a small table near the front door. A large oblong table with an oil cloth spread and a kerosene lamp on it stood opposite the range, and there were chairs drawn up under it and placed about the room.

The upstairs rooms had slanting ceilings and one window each in their gable ends. Mama and Pa slept in one of the rooms. The four girls slept in the other. The boy slept downstairs on the davenport.

The boy was anxiously counting the days until Christmas. He wanted a train. He had pored over the pages of toy trains in the Montgomery Ward catalog that came to his house and in the Sears and Roebuck catalog at Grandpa's house up the road until he could see the pictures when he closed his eyes and could nearly recite the descriptions from memory.

As the oldest of the five children — who in a few years would be increased by the births of two more boys to seven — he had an edge on his sisters in Christmas experiences. Most of his experiences had been happy ones but he had known disappointments and somehow he felt he might be disappointed again.

A train. He had to have a train for Christmas. He had to find a way to make sure Santa Claus understood that. He had seen exactly what he wanted in the catalogs. It was a deluxe set with freight cars, a guaranteed spring-driven engine, two switches, a siding and a miniature station and signals. If he could just get that he wouldn't want anything else. Nothing else, Santa Claus, just that train with switches.

But there were rules: You didn't get what you wanted for Christmas unless you were good. Santa Claus kept a list and everything bad you did was written in it. The boy shuddered to think of that. He could only anxiously hope Santa Claus might forgive and forget if he would be really good from now until Christmas Eve.

The girls always seemed to be good and he seemed always to be getting into trouble. He didn't mean to be bad but things were always happening that turned out to be his fault.

Like getting into things that didn't belong to him, or bothering things that should be left alone, or misplacing Pa's tools, or rummaging in Mama's sewing machine drawers and losing her needles. Or like using Pa's saw to cut a side of salt meat that shouldn't have been cut and then leaving the saw in the meat house to corrode.

If he had been a little older he might have understood his problem was acute curiosity and, understanding, might have known how to curb it.

He was still, though, a boy too little for rationalizations. He and his oldest sister Frances, a year younger than he, had just started to school the past September. He liked to read and write. But more than anything he liked to read things he shouldn't and open boxes and pull out drawers to see what had been added since the last time he had looked and to take things apart that usually he couldn't put back together.

A few weeks before Christmas, he and Frances had come home from school, walking the long road from the mail box by the frog pond where the school bus stopped, past the turn that led to Grandpa's and across the rude footbridge across the creek at the bottom of the ravine up the hill to the little house, and had found Mama and Pa and the three little sisters gone.

The boy and Frances cut pieces of the big homemade bread that Mama baked and made peanut butter sandwiches. After they had eaten and realized fully that they were the only ones at home, the boy without really thinking about it opened the door of the closet under the stairs.

There was nothing there but jars of vegetables his mother had put up from the garden and some old X-ray plates his father had brought home from the hospital to study. The boy puzzled over the X-rays for a while, then put them back in the closet and closed the door.

Next he opened the doors of the sideboard, listlessly examined the collection of bowls and whatnots his mother had stored and indifferently rummaged through the drawers. Nothing really interesting had been placed in the sideboard since the last time he had plundered it.

Finally, after a similar inspection of the kitchen cabinet, the ice box and the kitchen generally, he went upstairs. Since the upstairs closet was at the head of the stairs, he looked into it before going into the bedrooms.

At the very back of the closet, harbored snug under the slanting eaves, was a large cardboard box. He had seen it many times before. It contained extra towels and out-of-season clothing and nothing at all exciting, at least not the last time he had gone through it.

Now, with nothing else to do but wait for his parents to return, he found himself mysteriously attracted by the big cardboard box. He pushed through the coats and dresses hanging at the front of the closet and worked himself up to the big box.

He pulled aside the old bedspread Mama had laid across it to keep dust from getting inside. He took out a layer of towels and reached to lift another layer. His hand felt something solid, somthing like a carton, something that hadn't been there before.

The boy reached into the big box with both hands and pulled out the carton and lifted it out. It was wrapped with brown paper and tied with a string. He carried the carton out to the tiny landing at the head of the stairs, cut the string with the knife he got from the kitchen and pulled away the wrapping paper.

255

The carton contained a baby doll.

The boy immediately plunged back into the closet.

He reached into the big cardboard box again and felt another and larger carton. It, too, was wrapped in brown paper and tied with a string. The boy cut the string and pulled off the wrapping paper. The carton was large and white and across the top was a big picture of a train — a passenger train. The words "American Flyer" were printed in large letters above the picture.

The boy opened the carton and in it found an engine and tender, three brightly painted tin passenger cars and a collection of track.

It wasn't a freight train. There weren't any switches. There was no miniature station or signals. It was a train, but it wasn't the train he wanted. It was a train, but whose train could it be?

The boy wondered if he should call his sister. He stiffled the impulse. Something told him he had discovered a secret that Frances mustn't know. Something told him he had discovered a secret he wished he didn't know.

He put the wrapping paper back around the carton not nearly as neatly as it had been wrapped about it originally. He tried to retie the string but, because he had cut it, it was too short to tie. He put the train back in the big cardboard box, realizing as he did so that there were other cartons there he might have examined. He rewrapped the baby doll in its carton and placed it in the big box not even bothering to retie the string about it. And when he had stuffed the towels back in place, he backed out of the closet and closed the door.

When he came downstairs again, he found Frances seated in the big imitation leather rocking chair studying her first grade reader.

"Where have you been?" she asked.

"Oh, just upstairs," he said.

"You better stay out of things up there," she said. "Mama told me none of us should do any rummaging or pulling out or we'd spoil our Christmas. She said if we did we'd really be sorry."

The boy couldn't think of an answer.

"I think I'll make me a cheese and mustard sandwich," he said.

"You'll spoil your supper," Frances told him.

"It's already spoiled," he said.

He went into the kitchen. He didn't make the cheese and mustard sandwich. Instead he closed the little door that led to the stairs and sat uphappily quiet on one of the kitchen chairs. Something was wrong. Doll babies and toy trains hidden in the upstairs closet. There had to be an explanation but he couldn't think of one.

All he could think of was that he wanted that freight train with the switches and the siding and the station and signals worse than anything he ever wanted before. The American Flyer passenger train in the closet was no substitute. He'd have to find a way to tell somebody. He supposed he'd have to write Santa Claus another letter, and maybe ought to tell Mama. But how could he do that without letting her know he'd been doing again something he shouldn't.

"Frances," he called from the kitchen, "do you think there really is a Santa Claus?"

"I think so," she said. "What do you think?"

And the boy answered dolefully, "I don't know. I just don't know. But if I don't get what I want for Christmas I'm going to give up believing."

The weeks until Christmas passed so slowly that the boy wondered if Christmas Eve would ever come. He worried and wondered about the big box in the closet. He worried about Santa Claus and he laboriously wrote several letters telling about the freight train in the catalog and making it clear that a passenger train wouldn't do. He addressed the letters to the North Pole and gave them to his mother to mail.

On Christmas morning the boy was the first out of bed. He scrambled from under the covers and off the davenport and ran to the Christmas tree.

There was a large box under the tree with a bright picture of a smoking train racing across it. Inside was a freight train — the very one he had seen in the catalog.

He took out the train and assembled the track.

Later when Mama came down with Pa, she looked at him and the train.

"Did Santa Claus bring you what you wanted?" she asked.

"Oh yes," he said happily. "A train exactly like I wanted, with everything I wanted."

"And I'll bet," she said with a sly smile," this is one Christmas you were really surprised."

There was something about the way Mama spoke that made him blush and that puzzled him. He had been surprised. And he was bewildered. And he was as happy in his bewilderment as he ever had been before in all the eight Christmases of his life.

"CHRISTMAS GIFT"

Christmas was wonderfully special at Grandfather's house. Grandfather was Josephus Daniels, the famous Tar Heel editor, who served his country as Secretary of the Navy in Wilson's Cabinet and Ambassador to Mexico under Roosevelt and loved Christmas as much as he loved North Carolina and his family.

By Lucy Daniels Inman

"Christmas Gift! Give it to me!" My grandfather's face used to glow when he said that. His cheeks became shiny apples; his blue eyes flickered with merriment; and the white V-shaped scar on his forehead stretched to where it barely showed. His voice was exultant, and he laughed with such glee that everybody else had to laugh too.

"Christmas Gift! Give it to me!" We children wondered at that greeting which was so foreign to us. Old fashioned, we called it, and decided pityingly that Grandfather had grown up before the days of "Merry Christmas!"

Still more tragic, he had only a meagre knowledge of Santa Claus. He knew who he was, of course, and even discussed him with us occasionally. But Grandfather seemed to have had little personal experience with the jolly benefactor of Christmas night.

We gathered this chiefly from a story he told about receiving a new dime for Christmas the year he was five. He said he had treasured that dime: "The sun shone upon it and made it look more beautiful than anything I thought I had ever seen. I felt richer that day than I have ever felt since, and I would run my hand in my pocket and hold that dime up to the sun again and again."

That story worried us. If Santa Claus visited every child in the world on Christmas Eve, how had he missed Grandfather? We found it difficult to believe that this dignified white-haired old man had ever been a little boy. But if he had, surely he had not been bad enough to displease Santa Claus. If one of us had received only a dime for Christmas, we would have felt grossly mistreated.

The only suitable explanation we ever found for this was the one we employed for many other things about Grandfather. He was simply different from anyone else in the whole world.

My grandmother was different, too — but chiefly because she was a part of Grandfather. For the most part, she was both a gracious lady and a warm, not too perfect human being. The governing fire of her life was the blend of love and respect she had for her husband. She never called him anything but "Mr. Daniels." Yet, I doubt if even she knew the extent to which she molded his life.

"Nanny" was already growing old when I first knew her. She was a too-plump pigeon of a woman with soft white hair and blue eyes that could either sparkle or go deliberately blank. She had a smile of sunshine and a will of iron. And though selfish in the way many mothers are selfish, she also possessed a boundless generosity. Confined to a wheel chair by the heart condition of which she eventually died, she had a firm belief in — and perhaps too keen an appetite for — the good things in life. She extended this to the lives of others.

Together, she and Grandfather always made their own special kind of Christmas. I'm sure they did not regard it as unique, and, in fact, it contained many of the traditional elements. The holly and mistletoe, the shining tree, gifts and carol singing, turkey and plum pudding. And the additional features were not such that they altered the spirit of the occasion.

The real difference was something bigger and less tangible than the image we children had of Santa Claus and the Christ Child. I'm not even sure that difference can be described by words. Generosity might do it partially. But only if you consider generosity universal, including self as well as the rest of the world. Only if you think of it as gay as well as good.

Sometimes in the heat of a fight over a Christmas toy Grandfather would say, "Remember, It's more blessed to give than to receive." That was close to the essence of Christmas in that house. But not if given its usual connotation. Not unless you can forget to say, "That's in the Bible. Jesus said that." Though I'm sure both Nanny and Grandfather thought of that when they quoted it, I doubt if they knew they lived by it. They gave mountains of gifts each year — not just to their children and grandchildren, but to servants and servants' children, to some people they didn't even know, and to others whom they knew to be less fortunate than they, in money or happiness.

Part of this, I'm sure, was due to Nanny's desire to be a gracious benevolent lady. And part to Grandfather's drive to make up for the enforced frugality of his youth. Perhaps, too, they were assuaging some guilt feelings for having so much in a world that had so little. But their giving went far beyond all that. As they practiced it, "It is more blessed to give than to receive," meant "Giving is fun." They gave presents simply because it gave them pleasure to do so – a pleasure similar to that Nanny felt in seeing other people devour the rich foods the doctors forbade her. In no altruistic or pious sense, they were happy when they saw others happy. It was fun.

And apparently for them the gift was its own reward. Their happiness was not dependent on any show of gratitude from the recipient. Undoubtedly it pleased them to see one of us children particularly thrilled over a gift. But they appeared equally delighted when they gave us government savings bond — one gift which we valued little and often forgot to thank them for.

Christmas was a big, big time in our world and the festivities at Nanny's and Grandfather's only a part of it. The noises — jangling bells, rustling tissue paper, furtive whispering. The smells — green pine, cookies baking, turkey roasting, the turpentine used in painting pine cones. But best of all, that Christmas feeling. So many sensations and partial sensations. Excitement, happiness, wonder. Perhaps even a little holiness and tranquility.

All this began with the last bowl of soup made from the Thanksgiving turkey and reached its peak with the celebration at Nanny's and Grandfather's on Christmas Day. And two important images filled the days between — Santa Claus with his sleigh full of toys and the Christ Child who emerged so magically real from our mother's blue and gold book. Each of these was as wonderful as the other; each completely unanswerable and at the same time unquestioned by us.

In our everyday lives Grandfather, alone, came close to combining these two ideas. He could be both good and merry. He could shout "Christmas Gift!" even when he thought, "It is more blessed to give than to receive." In even my earliest recollections of him, Grandfather was an old man. He walked with a cane, and the hand he waved in greeting was too stiff to open flat. His face was textured with the fine webbed etchings of time. But he was to me — and, I imagine, to most of his grandchildren — not only *an* old man, but *the* old man who was forever young.

Now, sometimes, I remember that he was the second son of a poor ship carpenter's widow, raised in the hard years after the Civil War. And I am proud of the way he worked up from that to a good and productive life not only for himself, but for his state and for his world. I have heard and read about his bitter conflicts with various men, and I can often see his opponents' sides. Not then, though. To me as a little girl, if Grandfather had enemies, they were both wicked and stupid, the kind of people who would antagonize God and Santa Claus.

So, each year we had the luxury of a double Christmas. The one at home, and the more magnificent one at Nanny's and Grandfather's. Besides the gifts and the holly and the shining tree, which we all knew Grandfather had been too busy to think about until the moment we arrived, there was the massive dining rom table loaded with food. Too much food — in both quantity and variety. Turkey, ham, beaten biscuits, risen biscuits, hot rolls, rice and gravy, five or six vegetables, pickles, fruit, plum pudding, mince pie, ice cream and fruitcake. All the things Nanny loved and should not eat — but did. And though we stuffed ourselves until our mothers admonished us about stomach aches, that feast appeared barely touched when we stood up from the table. All to the good since there were five servants in the kitchen to take it home with them.

We came to count on that celebration at the big house — as much on Grandfather's gaiety as on Nanny's banquet. Yes, we counted on it, and it came without fail year after year — the gifts and the laughter and the singing, the feast and "Christmas Gift!"

Until 1943, the year Nanny died.

There was no Christmas that year. The country was at war, and because of it, my mother and my sisters and I remained in Washington, D. C. Only my father came home to Raleigh that Christmas. And not for the big dinner and the carol singing; just to be on hand for the arrival of death.

We children were greatly saddened by that. It was our first experience with death, and our first realization that the things we treasured were not immortal. But for us the hurt healed quickly, and by the next fall we talked eagerly again of Grandfather's Christmas.

The grownups said we would not go home. The Christmas festivities had been Nanny's project. Grandfather, with all his work and the weight of his sadness, could not be expected to carry on the tradition. We were growing up then, becoming reconciled to reality. With sadness but little disbelief, we accepted the explanation that Nanny's Christmases were a thing of the past, that they could never be the same again. . .

But then something happened. I have never known what or how. But suddenly we *were* going to Grandfather's for Christmas. . . The grownups had been right, of course. It was not truly the same. The tree was just as tall and shining; the gifts under it just as numerous; the dinner table just as overladen with food. But also, there was an emptiness, through all the gaiety a silence.

Still, it *was* Christmas. And not just a stiff-upper-lip pretense to cheer a lonely old man. In fact, if anything, it was Grandfather who cheered us. He talked of Nanny as if she were in the next room. He told stories about when they had been young together. But warmly, never tragically, often laughing gaily.

And always, every year of his life after that, with the holly berries glistening in the sun or when the lamps were lit to guide us homeward, there was that exultant cry of "Christmas Gift! Give it to me!" Tears crowd my throat when I remember that now. But fast upon them comes the laughter — the deep, contagious ripple of merriment, which is as immortal for me as Christmas itself.

December 1969

THE BEST MEDICINE FOR CHRISTMAS

When families reunite in the old homes of North
Carolina for Christmas dinner, there are white-haired men
and women who look down the table at beaming
grandchildren and say the magic words:

"You don't know what it means to have everybody
well."

Happily, there aren't many children today who know
the significance of the homely pronouncement.

Of course, children still take sick and parents still tend
to equate winter with colds, earaches and sore throats, but
not as many families now seem to suffer the long sieges of
illness that so often used to spoil Christmas.

Only 40 years or so ago, when families were larger, at
least one of the children in the average home would be too
sick to get out of bed for Christmas. Between the beginning
of cold weather and the spring thaws it was not unusual for
every child in the house to be stricken with some winter
ailment, and those who came through a winter without
falling victim to the flu or worse were exceptionally lucky.

So when grandfathers and grandmothers speak so
fervently of the blessedness of having everybody well and
how nice it is that everybody can be together, perhaps only
they and their now middle-aged sons and daughters can
appreciate the deeper meaning of the words.

In the drafty houses of their time, when a child became
sick it had to be moved from the cold bedroom it shared
with its sisters or brothers. Often a temporary bed would
be improvised by placing two chairs together close to the
stove in what would now be called the family room so the
small patient could be kept warm.

Only those who experienced it can remember the mustard plasters, enemas, poultices, camphorated oil, spoonfuls of kerosene and sugar, hot flannels for chests and the other remedies used so desperately in the days before wonder drugs when mothers and fathers would spend the nights in sleepless, anxious vigils waiting for the fever to break.

Curiously, the old remedies usually worked. But it well may be it was not the medicines but the love and prayers of the parents who administered them that brought the cure. And it is important to remember that at Christmas time, because love and prayers make Christmas better, too.

A NEW BEGINNING

A fresh snow, a sudden thaw,
    a freeze,
All these in January. All these and
    more.
To make our Januarys full, and
    give us
Pause for reckoning and making
    plans
In the birth of a new year, that
    we may
Reshape our lives in a new beginning.
All these, the snow, the thaw, the
    ice.
The cold winds shaking at the
    windows,
The brown fields, gray winter
    skies,
The squirrel foraging, the birds
That should have gone but stayed,
Searching table scraps and
crumbs,
As we, with our resolutions, search
To start anew, to seek,
In the birth of a new year,
To find in January
A better way.

Jim Chaney, editor of *Carolina Country* and author of many of the selections in *Carolina Country Reader*, came to North Carolina in early 1942 to work in the Raleigh bureau of United Press.

He was a combat correspondent in World War II and later an award-winning reporter for *The News and Observer*. Before retiring from the Raleigh newspaper, he was also its Sunday editor and book editor. He became editor of *Carolina Country* (then known as *The Carolina Farmer*) in February 1967.

He is married to the former Janie Young Husketh of Kittrell. They have two children — Catherine, a graduate student at the UNC School of Public Health, and Jimmy, a student at Holding Tech.

Sam Ragan, guiding spirit in the publication of *Carolina Country Reader* and author of its foreword, is editor and publisher of *The Pilot* of Southern Pines and former executive editor of *The News and Observer*.

His weekly column, "Southern Accent," is known throughout North Carolina as a witty, perceptive and erudite commentary on books, writing, people, public affairs and the North Carolina scene. He has helped launch some of the nation's top journalists on their careers. Tar Heel writers and poets know him for his creative writing classes and workshops and as a friend and constructive critic.

He served as North Carolina's first Secretary of Art, Culture and History and is the author of two award-winning books of poetry — *The Tree In the Far Pasture* and *To the Water's Edge*. He is also the author of the book, *Free Press and Fair Trial; Dixie Looked Away*, an analysis of the 1964 election, and, with Elizabeth S. Ives, a book on Adlai Stevenson, *Back to the Beginnings*.

He is past president of the Associated Press Managing Editors Association, a former director of the American Society of Newspaper Editors and the current president of the North Carolina Press Association.

He and his wife Marjorie, associate editor of *The Pilot*, have two daughters, Nancy and Talmadge.